FIFTY PLACES TO ROCK CLIMB

BEFORE YOU DIE

FIFTY PLACES TO
ROCK CLIMB
BEFORE YOU DIE

Climbing Experts Share
the World's Greatest Destinations

Chris Santella

FOREWORD BY TIMY FAIRFIELD

ABRAMS IMAGE
NEW YORK

This book is for my girls, Cassidy, Annabel, and Deidre,
and for everyone who's ever sought inspiration in the vertical realm.

Fifty Places to Surf Before You Die

Fifty Places to Run Before You Die

Fifty Places to Drink Beer Before You Die

Fifty Places to Camp Before You Die

Fifty Places to Paddle Before You Die

Fifty Places to Bike Before You Die

Fifty Places to Fly Fish Before You Die

Fifty More Places to Fly Fish Before You Die

Fifty Places to Ski & Snowboard Before You Die

Fifty Places to Sail Before You Die

Fifty Places to Go Birding Before You Die

Fifty Places to Dive Before You Die

Fifty Places to Hike Before You Die

Fifty Places to Play Golf Before You Die

Fifty More Places to Play Golf Before You Die

Once in a Lifetime Trips:
The World's Fifty Most Extraordinary
and Memorable Travel Experiences

Fifty Favorite Fly-Fishing Tales:
Expert Fly Anglers Share Stories from the Sea and Stream

Why I Fly Fish:
Passionate Anglers on the Pastime's Appeal
and How It Has Shaped Their Lives

The Hatch Is On!

The Tug Is the Drug

CAT WARS (with Dr. Peter Marra)

Contents

Acknowledgments 9 / Foreword 11 / Introduction 13

THE DESTINATIONS

ACKNOWLEDGMENTS

This book would not have been possible without the generous assistance of the climbers who shared their time and experience to help bring these fifty great climbing venues to life. To these men and women, I offer the most heartfelt thanks. A special thanks goes out to Timy Fairfield, Francis Sanzaro, and Scott Stevens, who kindly made introductions on my behalf. I also want to acknowledge the fine efforts of my agent, Stephanie Kip Rostan; my editors Ashley Albert, Samantha Weiner, and Annalea Manalili; designer Anna Christian; and copy editor Margaret Moore who helped bring the book into being. Finally, I want to extend a special thanks to my wife, Deidre, and my daughters, Cassidy and Annabel, for their patience with my peripatetic lifestyle . . . and to my parents, Tina and Andy, who though passed now, always encouraged me to pursue my passions.

OPPOSITE: Germany's Frankenjura was the chosen home of Wolfgang Güllich, one of the world's greatest climbers.

9

FOREWORD

Growing up in the shadows of the Sandia Mountains, a dramatically uplifted fault ominously defining the eastern boundary of the city of Albuquerque, New Mexico, embedded the mysterious allure of rock climbing in my psyche as far back as I can remember. The most distinctive features of these rugged mountains are the proudly exhibited miles of granite big-wall pinnacles, the endless granite boulder fields dispersed throughout the foothills, and the network of inconspicuous steep limestone power bands—offering the potential for a lifetime of discovery.

I was fortunate enough to have been introduced to the mountains by my uncle Raymond, who brought me and my younger brother on a mini-expedition that consisted of setting our objective, planning the itinerary, preparing snacks, packing our climbing gear, sneaking out of the house without my mother noticing, orienteering the approach, exploring the boulder fields along the way, stopping for many snacks, locating the climb, route reading the line, being dragged up a little frozen waterfall, and getting our butts home before my mother found out! Pulling off such a scheme (even though we eventually got busted by Mom) signified a rite of passage for me as a person. I may not have been an adult yet, but I was "not a baby" anymore.

Being involved with rock climbing has provided me with tremendous personal and professional opportunities. I have traveled to more than forty countries, learned several languages, and cultivated meaningful personal relationships with incredibly diverse people who share the same underlying core human values and passion. Such experiences have helped me become a more complete human being and have contributed to my developing a global mind-set as a citizen of the world. My life experiences motivated by rock climbing have empowered me to think for myself, question authority, and dissent from the constructs of the privileged First World psychology, media distortion, social injustice, racial prejudices, and political dogma—leaving me with an unwavering and empathetic respect for all ethnicities, cultures, and peoples of the world.

I have met some of the most fascinating, personally evolved, and cultured individuals I know through climbing. I discovered my soul mate—with whom I have been in a relationship for almost two decades—through climbing competitions. We even found our dog on a climbing trip. I guess one could say that the yield has been high!

OPPOSITE:
Liming pioneer Mike Dobie sinks two fingers into the thin crack known as Wild Man Variation (5.12) on the multi-pitch classic Back to the Primitive—one of the must-do climbs in Liming, China.

11

Rock climbing has emerged as the most accessible and widely practiced sub-specialty from the family of disciplines sharing a common mountaineering lineage background. Collectively, all forms of rock climbing have experienced rapid and sustainable growth rates over the past few decades, even when compared with other outdoor action sports. Despite the persistently nebulous identity of rock climbing and the seemingly endemic absence of being acknowledged as a real "sport" for many decades, rock climbing is decisively revealing with style why it is worthy of such recognition.

Along with the maturation of the sport, the proliferation of indoor commercial climbing gyms, imminent Olympic inclusion, and the corresponding accelerated industry growth, outdoor rock climbing areas have become even more numerous, more varied in style, more impressive, and more widespread worldwide. When I first started climbing in the 1980s, there wasn't a single commercial climbing gym in North America. Since that time, North America has witnessed the launch of hundreds of commercial climbing gyms and thousands more institutional climbing-wall installations. The public is finally starting to realize that rock climbing isn't as dangerous as it is fun. As a result, climbing has risen to become one of the most compelling multifaceted sports in the world. Quite simply, the writing is on the wall.

The iconic climbing areas depicted by Chris Santella in *Fifty Places to Rock Climb Before You Die* will arouse a desire to discover yourself through the exploration of the world in pursuit of these awe-inspiring locations. Each is characterized by the uniqueness of its location, distinguishing geologic characteristics, and expressive climbing movement style. These areas are a reflection of the rich history, unique subculture, and dynamic direction of our young sport. Rock climbing is a mentally engaging, physically challenging, travel-based activity through which you may discover that there is much more human and athletic potential within yourself than you had ever thought possible. May this compilation of world-class climbing areas evoke a renaissance of ideas and inspire us to live with passion through experiencing rock climbing around the planet.

—Timy Fairfield
Albuquerque, New Mexico
President, Futurist Climbing Consultants, Inc.
Veteran, U.S. National Climbing Team
National and international climbing competition winner

INTRODUCTION

The world's earliest civilizations made rocks the centerpiece of their religions.

Our ancestors were on to something!

Rock climbing—be it in a gym, over boulders, on bolted sport crags or massive massifs—is experiencing an unprecedented surge in popularity that would have early "dirtbag" climbers tangled in their ropes. There are many good reasons. Rock climbing is incredible exercise. It hones mental focus, and trains us to set goals and prepare a path to meet them. It can be an opportunity to commingle with friends new and old or spend quiet quality time with a trusted climbing partner. And it can satisfy the timeless human desire to ascend into the sky and achieve a sense of liberation from gravity and the land below. Humans can't quite fly (at least not on their own), but climbing puts us a bit closer to the heavens . . . at least until it's time to rappel down.

I wrote *Fifty Places to Rock Climb Before You Die* for those adventurous climbers—from aspiring Stone Masters to weekend warriors—who are ever-ready to chalk up and scamper off to the next crag, cliff, or boulder.

"What makes a destination a place to climb before you die?" you might ask. The chance to follow the path of pioneering climbers on the world's most challenging routes? The opportunity to explore an unfamiliar region or country from the unique perspective offered from its limestone crags or granite walls? A chance to immerse yourself in the beauty of stunning natural settings while pushing past physical boundaries? Or simply the opportunity to share beta and stories with like-minded people who beyond the rocks might lead very different lives than you. The answer would be yes to all of the above, and an abundance of other criteria.

One thing I knew when I began this project: I was *NOT* the person to assemble this list. So I followed the recipe that served me well in my first fifteen *Fifty Places* books—to seek the advice of some talented and committed climbers. To write *Fifty Places to Rock Climb Before You Die*, I interviewed a host of people closely connected with the climbing world and asked them to share some of their favorite experiences—in trad climbing, sport climbing, and bouldering. These experts range from celebrated climbing professionals (like Kevin Jorgeson and Nina Caprez) to writers (like Matt Samet and Francis

Sanzaro) to employees of leading climbing companies (like Petzl and Black Diamond Equipment). Some spoke of venues that are near and dear to their hearts, places where they've built their professional reputations; others spoke of places they've visited only once but that made a profound impression. People appreciate climbing for many different reasons, and this range of attractions is evidenced here. (To give a sense of the breadth of the interviewees' backgrounds, a bio of each individual is included after each essay.)

Rock climbing means different things to different people. For some, it may mean working for weeks (or months) to tackle a vexing bouldering problem; for others, it may mean scaling multi-pitch walls sure to give the casual passerby a case of vertigo. *Fifty Places to Rock Climb Before You Die* attempts to capture the full spectrum of climbing experiences. While the book collects fifty great venues, it by no means attempts to rank the places discussed. Such ranking is, of course, largely subjective.

In the hope that a few readers might use this book as a guide for embarking on their own climbing adventures, I have provided brief "If You Go" information at the end of each chapter, including available guide services, guidebooks, and camping or lodging options. It's by no means a comprehensive list but should give would-be travelers a starting point for planning their trip.

Some climbers take great joy in learning the ins and outs of a favorite local crag. Yet a trip to a dream venue can forge memories to last a lifetime. It's my hope that this little book will inspire you to embark on some new climbing adventures of your own.

OPPOSITE: Rätikon is the centerpiece of Swiss rock climbing. NEXT PAGE: A climber and the park's eponymous tree at Joshua Tree National Park.

The Destinations

HORSE PENS 40

RECOMMENDED BY **Dylan Reingold**

The mountains of Alabama may not find themselves on too many must-visit lists for sport or trad climbing enthusiasts (though the Appalachians begin in the state's northeast corner). But its bouldering potential—in the shape of Horse Pens 40—draws die-hard enthusiasts from far and wide.

"I went to Horse Pens the first time in 2005," Dylan Reingold began. "I heard about the Triple Crown Bouldering Series [which is comprised of three Southern venues known as Horse Pens 40, Hound Ears, and Stone Fort] when I moved up to Jacksonville from Miami; Jacksonville was much closer to climbing venues in the Southeast, so I signed up for the series. I missed the first event at Hound Ears in Boone, North Carolina, but was able to make it to Horse Pens. After visiting a friend in Birmingham, I drove up to Steele, Alabama, with no knowledge about what I was getting into. It was a fantastic day. Much of my bouldering at that point had been indoors, so I struggled at first in the outdoor setting. But I was quickly befriended by some other competitors and climbed with them all day; one of those climbers became one of my best friends. I must have climbed—or attempted to climb—twenty-five problems. I was struggling with V0 problems at first, but eventually finished with several V2s. I loved the crowd, the energy, and the amazing rocks. And to top it all off, I came in second place in the beginner category! Since that visit, I've only missed one Triple Crown competition at Horse Pens."

Horse Pens 40 sits roughly an hour east of Birmingham, atop Chandler Mountain near the town of Steele. The rocks here date back as far as 1.3 billion years ago. Horse Pens takes its curious name from the property's official filing by its homesteader, John Hyatt, who referenced "the home 40, the farming 40, and the horse pens 40, each tract containing 40 acres of land." Though Hyatt was the first official homesteader, the sand-

OPPOSITE:
Antonio Carion
works Chicks
on Horse Pens'
Millipede boulder.

19

stone rock formations here have attracted humans for thousands of years. Some Native American peoples—including the Creeks and Cherokees—used the rocks around Horse Pens 40 for ceremonies. In more recent times, the dense array of boulders here has served as a hiding place for Cherokees (during the Trail of Tears forced relocation), Confederate soldiers, moonshiners, and outlaws. These days, Horse Pens primarily draws bluegrass fans for several annual festivals, and boulderers, who flock here during the cooler months to do battle with hundreds of problems, all linked by six miles of trails.

The explosion of interest in bouldering over the past twenty-five years would suggest that it's a fairly recent discipline, though in truth, it dates back to the late 1800s, when alpine rock climbing emerged as a sport. In its early days, bouldering was considered a way to stay in shape for more "serious" mountain adventures. It gained credibility as a sport unto itself as climbers in France in the 1930s—particularly around Fontainebleau—began tackling harder problems with innovative climbing techniques. Bouldering was further legitimized in the 1950s and '60s when John Gill began applying the skills he'd learned as a gymnast to increasingly difficult problems. In the early 1990s, when John Sherman developed the "V-scale" for his guidebook on Hueco Tanks in Texas, bouldering began gaining more popularity—and continues to, as evidenced by the many gyms springing up around the world that are devoted solely to bouldering.

There are many qualities that make Horse Pens 40 special—a great number of problems ranging from V0 to V12 to satisfy boulderers of all abilities, a pleasing rural setting, and great camaraderie, especially during the Triple Crown event. For many, it's Horse Pens' slopers that make it stand out. "It's squeeze compression climbing at its best," Dylan continued. "Take one of the great classics there, Bumboy. It's about slapping the rock. You can't dig your hands in. You slap, squeeze, move your body up. Slap, squeeze, and move your body up. There's a point when you get your hands slapped high enough on the rock that you know you're going to finish the climb; before that, you don't feel like you've got enough weight over the top. It's my understanding that Bumboy was once a V5, but since people have done it so much, it's been downgraded to a V3. There are other classics in the V2 to V4 range. Another that stands out for me is Earth, Wind & Fire. It's almost a crack climb. There's one really cool move you need to complete—you need to get your left hand in a feature horizontally so you can do a hand-foot match. That's the picture most people take. It gets really tall, and you're never completely comfortable up there. It's a very exciting finish when you catch the horn."

Horse Pens 40 is especially well suited to hosting a leg of the Triple Crown of Bouldering, a series of events that was created to raise funds for the Southeastern Climbers Coalition and the Carolina Climbers Coalition, and to provide a showcase for vendors serving the bouldering community. "There's a camping area where many climbers will pitch their tents, a restaurant, and a pavilion where vendors set up, and they hold the awards ceremony," Dylan described. "The competitive environment pushes you to climb a bit harder than you might otherwise."

It must work. In 2018, Dylan Reingold came in second place overall in the "Stonemaster" (age forty-five and over) category.

DYLAN REINGOLD is county attorney for Indian River County in Florida. His climbing adventures have taken him throughout the United States, including Devils Tower, Joshua Tree, Mount Rainier, Yosemite, the Red River Gorge, and the Shawangunks. When he's not climbing or helping to guide his county forward, Dylan enjoys running, reading, and going on cruises with his wife.

If You Go

▶ **Getting There:** Steele is about an hour northeast of Birmingham, which is served by most major carriers.

▶ **Best Time to Visit:** Fall through early spring provides the best climbing conditions; according to Dylan, "the slap and squeeze works best when it's cooler." There's a modest fee for park access (detailed at www.hp40.com).

▶ **Level of Difficulty:** There's everything from V0 to V12 here, with a great assemblage of intermediate problems. Pads and shoes are available for rent for beginners.

▶ **Guides:** No guide services are available in Steele, though Adam Henry's guidebook *Horse Pens 40 Bouldering* will point you in the right direction.

▶ **Accommodations:** Camping is available at Horse Pens 40 (www.hp40.com), and there are several rustic cabins on the property. There are several chain motels in nearby Gadsden.

BOW RIVER VALLEY

RECOMMENDED BY **Ellen Powick**

The Bow River Valley—both inside and outside of Banff National Park—provides one of the most beautiful alpine settings in the world, and a variety of excellent rock climbing opportunities. But for Ellen Powick, its appeals were not immediately obvious. "I grew up in nearby Calgary and as a kid was not really an outdoorsy person," she began. "As they say, you don't fully appreciate a place until you move away. Well, I moved east for university and realized how great the west was. Then I got introduced to climbing in my mid-twenties and started to spend time exploring climbing areas around Canmore. I mostly sport climb, but I do enjoy some traditional and multi-pitch climbing as well. At the time, there was already a fair amount of development, and it was a great place to cultivate my skills. However, it still seemed like there was more climbing, better climbing, and a longer rock season elsewhere, so after my husband and I got married, we took a year off work and explored the United States for climbing. We became more competent climbers and ended up moving to Utah so that we could take advantage of climbing year-round. Twenty-four years later I am still as obsessed and passionate about climbing as ever. With family still in Calgary, I visit every summer and I take the time to climb in the Bow River Valley while I am there. Over the past ten years, there's been a lot of climbing development, so there are always some new climbs to check out when I visit. I have to say that the Canadian Rockies are a great escape from 100-degree summer temperatures back home in Utah."

Canmore rests roughly fifty miles west of Calgary, and a few miles shy of the east entrance to Banff National Park. The region from Canmore through Banff on to Jasper is marked by incredibly scenic valleys, meadows, glaciers, icefields, and mountains; driving the Icefields Parkway that connects Banff with Jasper National Park to the north, it seems the vista at each turn is the most beautiful you've ever witnessed . . . until you reach the

OPPOSITE: Climber Kris Irwin takes in the view of Lake Louise in Alberta's Banff National Park on Back in the Saddle (5.11b).

next bend! Wildlife is also abundant, including black and grizzly bear, elk, moose, caribou, bighorn sheep, and wolves. The area around Canmore and Banff National Park came to be known as an outdoor recreation paradise thanks in large part to the Canadian Pacific Railway. The railroad, completed in 1885, created a supply of westbound train seats from the eastern population centers; the railway did not underestimate the region's appeal, and it soon gained an international reputation.

While hikers and sightseers are drawn to Banff, climbers tend to focus their energies on the many crags around Canmore—in large part, because much of the rock in Banff is of less than exceptional quality. In fact, it's been said that Banff has the worst rock in North America that still gets climbed, though there are certainly notable exceptions, like the quartzite at the Back of Lake Louise and the dolomite at Castle Mountain. "The rock is mainly limestone around Canmore," Ellen continued, "so the sport climbing is amazing, especially in the harder grades. Recently, there's been a lot of multi-pitch development in the area, particularly in moderate grades, so there is something for everyone."

Of the 25-plus crags around Canmore, Acéphale is one of the most beloved. A mix of blue and gray limestone, it offers up forty-five routes, mostly 5.12 and above, split between two sectors. "The Lower and Upper Wall have different styles, but are both excellent," Ellen enthused. "There are many, many good routes to choose from." The Lower Wall tends to have a bit more variety and attainable grades; the Upper offers more powerful, intense climbs, including several of the hardest routes in the Canmore area. Echo Canyon is another favorite, with more than 140 bolted routes and more still being developed. "One of my favorite walls there is Atlantis at the Lookout sector," she said. "I love the routes here—blocky, with pinches that make it sometimes feel like Rifle Canyon back in Colorado, only far from the road and not as greasy. I also like the Planet X Wall in Cougar Canyon. My favorite route there is Shooting Star, a classic 5.12d. It's worth mentioning that the crags around Canmore have a longer approach than most sport climbers are used to. Acéphale is forty-five minutes; some, like Echo Canyon, can be twice as long. Because of the length of the approach, we'll usually take a little time to cool off after the hike, and do a few easier climbs before tackling a project. Two or three burns on a project and it's usually time to quit, as the hikes out take longer than you'd expect."

While the Bow River Valley is best known for its sport climbing, there are certainly some worthy multi-pitch climbs. One that appeals to Ellen is Hoka Hey (5.9), on the South Peak of Mount Cory in Banff. "It's a 1,350-foot climb over nine pitches, and mostly bolt-protected," she described. "I also like Beautiful Century [5.10a], which is on the Nanny Goat crag. It's 750 feet over seven pitches, and it's also bolted." Bow River Valley climbers have also long looked to Yamnuska (also known as Mount John Laurie), one of the centers of Canadian Rockies trad climbing. This massif, just north of the Bow River, has more than two hundred lines, ranging from 5.4 to 5.13.

Should you choose to take a day off from the walls, many outdoor diversions await. Hiking in Banff is world class, and the Plain of the Six Glaciers trail, which heads at Lake Louise, is one of North America's great walks. For something a bit less strenuous, you could rent a canoe and paddle the lake's turquoise waters, or simply hoist an ale at the Lakeview Lounge at the Fairmont Chateau Lake Louise and take in the vistas.

ELLEN POWICK has been climbing since 1996 and has climbed routes to 5.14b. Her adventures have taken her across the United States, and abroad to Greece, Spain, France, Slovenia, and Switzerland. When she's not developing security software, Ellen's out on the rocks or training in the gym. A Canadian ex-pat, she lives in Utah with her husband, Kolin, and Labrador, Rumple.

If You Go

▶ **Getting There:** Calgary is roughly fifty miles from Canmore and served by many major carriers. Banff is another fifteen miles west from Canmore Road.

▶ **Best Time to Visit:** Climbing in lower elevation areas is possible from May to October. At elevations over eight thousand feet, the season is mid-June through September.

▶ **Level of Difficulty:** There's a range of options around Canmore and Banff for both sport and trad climbers.

▶ **Guides:** There are a number of guidebooks for the area, including *Bow Valley Sport* (Derek Galloway). Several guide services offer climbing; see a partial list at www.tourism canmore.com.

▶ **Accommodations:** The Alpine Club of Canada (www.alpineclubofcanada.ca) offers simple, affordable rooms. Tourism Canmore Kananaskis (www.tourismcanmore.com) lists motel, hotel, and camping options in the region.

FREY

Sometimes when plans change on an epic adventure, the trip is ruined. But sometimes, the traveler encounters unexpected treasures.

"I was on a climbing trip to Patagonia," Quentin L. Roberts recalled. "A friend and I had just climbed the south face of Fitz Roy. We were hoping to do more alpine climbing in that range, but the weather was forecast to be bad there. He suggested we visit Frey, which is sometimes used as a warm-up area for climbers heading to the taller and harder mountains, like those in Torres del Paine National Park or around El Chaltén. We made our way to the town of Bariloche [a hub city for outdoor adventurers—rather like Bozeman, Montana, or Bend, Oregon], and then hiked four hours into one of the most incredible camping areas I've ever seen. It's free, and sits nestled on the shores of an alpine lake surrounded by granite spires. We ended up spending two weeks there climbing. If I travel to climb, it's usually to big mountain ranges for alpine ascents. There aren't many places I'd travel to just to rock climb, but Frey is one of them."

Like Texas, Patagonia is as much a state of mind as a place. Encompassing roughly four hundred thousand square miles of infinite steppes, groaning glaciers, rugged pink granite peaks, and electric-blue lakes, wind-pummeled Patagonia is still very much a frontier. Frey is situated in the north of Argentine Patagonia in the Cerra Catedral region of Nahuel Huapi National Park. It takes its name from pioneering Argentine climber Emilio Frey, who served as park administrator of the Nahuel Huapi and co-founded the Club Andino Bariloche. Situated at an elevation of roughly 5,500 feet, Frey is made up of two connected alpine cirques, surrounded by spires offering one- to ten-pitch routes. Lake Toncek rests in the middle. A nearby *refugio* (simple lodge) offers travelers hearty hot meals and shelter, as well as free camping on the surrounding grounds. Though earlier

OPPOSITE: Frey near the town of Bariloche in northern Patagonia is a paradise of infinite spires.

27

European immigrants were among the first to climb around Frey in the early 1930s, its popularity increased after the Second World War when a new wave of immigrants arrived in Argentina.

A trip to Frey begins with the aforementioned hike, which starts near the Cerro Catedral ski resort. The trail climbs through a valley, over several rushing streams (spanned by sturdy footbridges), and through a thick forest before emerging above the tree line. "It's a fairly steep hike in," Quentin continued, "but it's a well-established trail. It's easy to navigate, and you can carry a massive backpack with lots of luxuries." Once you've set up your camp (or found your bunk in the refugio), you can begin to take in the many spires around you in all their magnificence, a wonderland of granite for trad climbers. "The climbs here encompass a huge range of difficulty—there's something for everyone," Quentin added. "But Frey still incorporates a bit of spice in the climbing, and I like that. Additionally, there are many interesting granite features. The weathering of the granite has created crazy holds, in combination with brilliant cracks." (While predominantly a trad climbing destination, portions of some popular routes are bolted.)

An hour or so chatting with fellow visitors at the Refugio Frey—perhaps over a bottle of local wine or mugs of mate tea—will begin to reveal the area's must-climb spires. Some conversations may mix in sign language and pantomime, as you're likely to encounter climbers from throughout South America and beyond at Frey. (The only printed source of information is a guide prepared by a fine local climber named Rolando Garibotti; his hand-drawn topographic maps can also be found online.) Some of the spires are a short walk from the refugio. Others can be up to a two-hour hike away. Torre Principal is the region's tallest spire, a golden granite monolith looming to the west of the lake, and two ascents here, Siniestro Total and No TEOlvidaremos, are among Frey's signature climbs. Siniestro (5.10+) is Frey's longest route, comprising of ten pitches on the west side of Torre Principal. (The fourth pitch may be the most exciting, a series of finger and hand cracks over almost one hundred feet.) TEO (5.12a) is named for Teo Plaza, who's considered one of Argentina's greatest—if not *the* greatest—climbers. (Sadly, Plaza perished in an avalanche; as Garibotti notes in a fine piece on Patagonia's contribution to climbing published in the magazine *Rock and Ice*, TEOlvidaremos is a play on the phrase "We will not forget you, Teo.") It's a five-pitch climb on the windy south side of Torre Principal, a delectable mix of face and crack climbing on an exquisitely clean piece of rock. The routes on Aguja Campanile Esloveno, Aguja Frey, and Aguja M2 also get high marks.

Though Frey offers world-class climbing, crowds are seldom a problem. In his two weeks there, Quentin never encountered more than twenty-five fellow climbers. But on one special day, it was nice to have a bit of company. "It was my climbing partner's birthday," he recalled. "We were climbing one spire, and our friend Brette [Harrington, another gifted young climber] was climbing another nearby spire by herself. We were hollering back and forth to each other, and we were the only people out there. As we summited, there were Andean condors [a member of the vulture family that boasts wing-spans in excess of ten feet] circling around the spires. It was spectacular."

QUENTIN L. ROBERTS grew up in the United Kingdom, Germany, South Africa, and British Columbia, and has always loved the mountains. His alpine climbing adventures have taken him through the United States, Asia, and South America. Quentin holds a degree in mechanical engineering, and when he's not climbing or cragging, he works in Vancouver at Conetec, a mining, geoenvironmental, and geotechnical site investigation contractor. He is sponsored by ARC'TERYX, La Sportiva, and Petzl.

If You Go

► **Getting There:** Most visitors will fly first to Buenos Aires and then on to Bariloche, which is served by several carriers, including LATAM Airlines (www.latam.com). It's a short bus ride to the trailhead at Cerro Catedral ski area, and then a four-hour hike in to Frey.

► **Best Time to Visit**: The austral summer, December through March, offers the best conditions.

► **Difficulty**: Most of the routes at Frey fall between 5.9 and 5.12, though some easier climbs are present.

► **Guides**: Several guides will lead excursions to Frey, including Andescross (530-448-8399; www.andescross.com). Rolando Garibotti's guidebook—available in Bariloche—will prove useful.

► **Accommodations**: Visitors to Frey can either camp or rent a bunk at Refugio Frey (www.clubandino.org). A number of hostels are available in Bariloche.

COCHISE STRONGHOLD

RECOMMENDED BY **Tanya Bok**

Cochise Stronghold is a bit off the radar for many in the climbing community. But those climbers who do know it covet the stronghold as a gem, a world-class destination.

"Cochise is known as a hardman area," Tanya Bok began. "There's the perception that it takes big *cojones* to climb, making people hesitant to visit. It's true that it's not easy to navigate Cochise's labyrinth of granite domes and tight gullies chocked with oak, manzanita, and alligator juniper. You're often alone out there, the approaches are longer, and if you get off track you might get little wounds from *Agave lechugilla* [Shin Dagger].

"While Cochise may not be ideal for new climbers, it can be a place that revives a sense of adventure for experienced climbers and a place of growth for any climber. I wrote my Cochise guidebooks to share what I have discovered and encourage others to step out of their comfort zones. Cochise challenges you and makes you question what you can and can't do. As you earn your chops on Cochise granite, you can graduate up to the big domes and historical routes. There are hundreds of places you can climb at Cochise, even if you're not a hardman. When I moved to Arizona, the Stronghold became my home more than my house in Tucson. At the center of our home, hundreds of feet high, granite domes are eroded out like slices of a gigantic bread loaf that act as our roof; in the valley, under a mantel created by a canopy of trees, a little patch of dirt next to a fire became our hearth. Everyone who visits Cochise should expect to leave some blood, sweat, and tears. But you'll also leave with a smile, and a little different than when you arrived."

Cochise Stronghold rests in the Dragoon Mountains of the Coronado National Forest, in the southeastern corner of Arizona. It's a fine example of a sky island habitat, rising to elevations of over five thousand feet from the surrounding desert. Thanks to the elevation, different flora and fauna thrive here among the woodlands, imposing

OPPOSITE: Cochise Stronghold is a celebrated "hardman" area near Tucson, Arizona. But with patience, it will reveal its wonders to less-seasoned climbers.

granite domes, and sheer cliffs. (The Stronghold takes its name from a Chiricahua Apache chief, Cochise, who bedeviled U.S. Army forces in the territory of present-day Arizona.)

While Cochise's warriors certainly scaled the formations around the Stronghold to monitor their enemies' movements, recreational climbers didn't begin exploring the area until the early 1970s. A leading pioneer was Dave Baker, who put up many classics at Cochise. Baker also established the area's first climbing shop, the Summit Hut, which provided a hub for the nascent Tucson climbing community. As Fitz Cahall notes in a fine *Climbing* piece on the Stronghold, the Summit Hut was also the repository of "a three-ring binder known as 'the Book' that held hand-drawn topos to all of southern Arizona; it passed from climber to climber until it finally disappeared."

Fortunately for climbers, much of the material from "the Book" materialized for Tanya. "I was cleaning out a filing cabinet, and I came across hundreds of hand-drawn topos and route descriptions for the Stronghold," Tanya wrote in a story for *Rock and Ice*. "I was also the holder of some of the original material used in Bob Kerry's *Backcountry Rock Climbing in Southern Arizona*. Mix this with new route development compiled from the intervening twenty years, and ten years of my personal climbing and route development, and I had a recipe for a guidebook."

Climbing at Cochise is divided between the East and West Strongholds; given their distance apart and the length of most approaches, climbers will generally commit to being on one side or the other. To Tanya, What's My Line (5.6+R, A0/5.10, on the southeast face of Cochise Dome in the East Stronghold) is as good an introduction as any to Stronghold climbing. "All that's sticking out of this seven hundred–foot face are chicken heads [a knob of rock, case-hardened and eroded out of the surrounding matrix]," she explained. "When I first climbed it, I had never encountered such a feature. Lots of newcomers look at it and think, 'Can I really just sling chicken heads all the way up?' But once they do, it resonates. You can see why this 'easy' route is considered a classic. I also like to send people to Endgame (5.10-, in the Rockfellow Group in the East Stronghold). The route sends you up a big dome, where each of the five pitches is different and requires different techniques. Some climbers who are comfortable with 5.10s will attempt a route like Endgame and say that Cochise is sandbagged. I think some of that perception comes from the foreboding nature of the place. It's intimidating and doesn't allow easy passage for all visitors, at least not with the first sampling."

Climbing satisfaction at Cochise can come from overcoming challenges, or from the self-reliance that comes from a successful backcountry expedition. Or, from simply absorbing the colors of a late afternoon. "The granite takes on glowing pink and golden hues, patched with chartreuse lichen," Tanya described. "The trees are a blue and green. It's a warm, soft color palette. Being among these granite domes you witness the swifts, turkey vultures, and peregrine falcons start patrolling the sky. Tired after a long day of climbing, I watch the sun slip below the horizon and saturate the sky in color so vibrant it seems artificial. It is here, I get a feeling I haven't found anywhere else."

TANYA BOK is a native of Alberta, a registered nurse by vocation, and a Cochise Stronghold devotee by avocation. She has rock climbed all over the United States and the Canadian Alpine, preferring long, remote climbs where the modern world does not reach her. This penchant drew her to explore the deep recesses of the Cochise Stronghold, climbing, developing routes, and painstakingly documenting, photographing, and designing two in-depth guidebooks on the area: *Cochise Stronghold: Rock Climbing on the West Side* and *Cochise Stronghold: Rock Climbing on the East Side* (www.cochiseclimbing.com).

If You Go

▶ **Getting There:** Cochise Stronghold is approximately eighty miles southeast of Tucson, which is served by many carriers.

▶ **Best Time to Visit**: September through May, though multiple elevations and exposures mean you can eke out climbing all year.

▶ **Level of Difficulty**: There are routes to suit climbers with a range of abilities—5.5 to 5.12—though anyone climbing Cochise should be self-sufficient in a wilderness setting.

▶ **Guides**: Tanya Bok has compiled two extensive guides to the area: *Cochise Stronghold: Rock Climbing on the West Side* and *Cochise Stronghold: Rock Climbing on the East Side*, as well as *Cochise Stronghold: Select Climbs.*

▶ **Accommodations**: Primitive camping on BLM/Forest Service land is available in both the West and East Strongholds. Lodging is available in the towns of Wilcox, Tombstone, and Benson.

MOUNT ARAPILES

RECOMMENDED BY **Chris Peisker**

Given Chris Peisker's first visit to Mount Arapiles, it's a wonder that he went back. "I started climbing in the Blue Mountains near Sydney," he recalled. "It's a softer sandstone. I'd been climbing for two years before I made it to Arapiles, and I had great expectations, as it was well known in the climbing scene. I found it much harder than I anticipated. It was hard to read the rock, and the holds were weird. I was climbing at 5.10 at the time, and I utterly failed at several routes at that grade that I thought I'd climb comfortably. Frankly, I got my ass kicked for four or five days.

"I went back to Sydney and was inspired to train harder. Six months later I came back, and my climbing had improved. I was much better prepared—both physically and psychologically. The rock at Arapiles—quartzitic sandstone—is very hard. It's comparable to the rock you find at the Shawangunks in New York. The mountain was on top of a volcanic intrusion, and it baked the rock; that's one reason it's so hard. It's not exactly slick, but smooth. It was once a sea cliff, and it was rounded out by the ocean over time."

Mount Arapiles sits some two hundred miles northwest of Melbourne, near the western edge of the state of Victoria. It rises 460 feet from the Wimmera plains and is roughly three miles long. (The Grampians, a much more significant mountain range that also has climbing opportunities, is thirty miles southeast.) Climbers began putting up routes here in the early 1960s, and by the 1970s, the mountain began receiving international attention. Chris went on to detail the qualities that make Arapiles so special. "There are more than four thousand climbs here, but they're all fairly contained," he continued. "You have routes from twenty meters to almost two hundred meters, from very easy to intermediate to really hard. There's a good distribution of climbs at all grades; on some faces, you'll have lower intermediate climbs right next to something extreme. Because of where

OPPOSITE:
Compact
Mount Arapiles
has more than
four thousand
routes for trad
climbers.

Arapiles is located—four hours from Melbourne and five hours from Adelaide—it's not very crowded. If it were two hours away from the cities, it would be overrun. Finally, this region of western Victoria has good weather. It's reasonably dry; but even if the weather is bad, it's usually only bad for a day."

With over forty years spent around Arapiles, Chris has experienced a good share of those four thousand routes. He divulged a few favorites. "Working as a guide for so many years, I've had the occasion to do a lot of easier climbs with beginners," he said. "My favorite easier route is Tiptoe Ridge. It's almost four hundred feet high, very steep at the top, but it's graded at 5.3. My daughter did it when she was three and a half . . . though she had a bit of experience, of course! Diaposon, in the Organ Pipes section, is another great easier climb, a 5.5. The Bard [5.6] is also a classic, a five-pitch that heads up a nose. Resignation, on the Tiger Wall, is another five-pitch climb that comes in at 5.7. It's one of the best routes at that grade. Skink, on the Right Watchtower Face, is a bit harder at 5.9, but a great climb. Second Coming [5.11b], on the Pharos, is a classic for the grade. When you get into the harder routes, the most iconic is Punks in the Gym. It was named and first sent by Wolfgang Güllich. When he put it up in 1985, it was the hardest climb that had ever been done, the first 5.14 in the world. Even today, thirty-four years later, there have probably been fewer than two hundred ascents. It's a beautiful line, going up a gently overhanging wall. When you look at it without chalk, it looks improbable. The rock looks incredibly smooth and rounded. There are holds there, but they're not obvious, and you can't see them from the ground."

There are motel and bed-and-breakfast accommodations in nearby towns, but if you want the full Arapiles experience, plan to pitch a tent at the Pines. "The camping is very good, not overly regulated," Chris described. "You pay your five dollars online and throw down a tent where you can find a piece of ground. Most of the routes are really close—within five or ten minutes. Even the longest approach is only thirty minutes, and the approaches are all flat. A lot of people will come in for a number of weeks, so real communities emerge. A lot of friendships are made here. There's only one thing you need to be careful of—slacklines. They are very popular with visitors, and if you're not cautious walking around at night, you could get garroted."

Chris spent a good deal of time at Mount Arapiles in the late 1970s . . . perhaps too much time. "I was living in a tent there between 1976 and 1979 for long stretches," he reminisced. "Almost two solid years. No one was there during the week, so I had the place more or less to myself. I'd welcome the weekends when a few people would show up to climb. I recall when I left in 1979. I was standing on the highway, trying to hitch a ride to Melbourne. I was so sick of the place. I didn't know if I'd ever see it again, and at that point, I didn't care. I never imagined I'd be back again in 1985. And now leading climbers has been my living for over thirty years."

Apparently the pull of that strange, isolated rock is strong.

CHRIS PEISKER has been climbing since he was a young boy and now has four decades of experience behind him. He has many first ascents to his name, including Australia's first grade 25 and the first grade 24 at Mount Arapiles. Chris was a key member in the founding of the Australian Climbing Instructors Association (ACIA) and has been the president for the past four years. He is still an active climber and instructor and believes climbing is a path to self-discovery. Chris owns and operates the Climbing Company in Natimuk, Victoria, which he founded in 1985.

If You Go

▶ **Getting There:** Melbourne is served by many major carriers from Los Angeles, including United (800-864-8331; www.united.com) and Quantas (800-227-4500; www.quantas .com). Arapiles is about a four-hour drive.

▶ **Best Time to Visit**: You can climb year-round at Arapiles, though austral summers (January and February) are hot. Autumn and spring are considered prime time.

▶ **Level of Difficulty**: Arapiles has everything from 5.3s to 5.14s.

▶ **Guides**: *Arapiles Selected Climbs* (Simon Mentz and Glenn Tempest) is the go-to guidebook. Several outfitters lead guided trips, including the Climbing Company (+61 35387 1329; www.climbco.com.au).

▶ **Accommodations**: The prime camping spot is the Pines in the Centenary Campground. You can reserve a site online at www.parkweb.vic.gov.au. The town of Horsham (www.visit horsham.com.au) has a number of lodging options.

INNSBRUCK

RECOMMENDED BY **Francis Sanzaro**

Winter Olympics aficionados of a certain age may recall the mountain-rimmed city of Innsbruck, which hosted the 1964 and 1976 games, as well as the 1984 and '88 Paralympic Games. With thousands of sport routes on a mix of limestone and granite crags in the surrounding hills, greater Innsbruck is the centerpiece of Austrian rock climbing. Yet for Francis Sanzaro, another of Innsbruck's main climbing attractions is just north of the Hofgarten, at Kletterzentrum Innsbruck—or the Innsbruck Climbing Center.

"I was born in 1979 and came of age as a climber in the early 1990s," he began. "At that time, indoor climbing in the United States was cultish. The gyms were dark, dingy places. I grew up in Baltimore, and to get to the local climbing gym, you had to take the light rail down to a postindustrial wasteland. It was an old warehouse that had been converted to a gym. I got hooked on gyms like this—it was rustic, raw, very counterculture. You didn't take your mom there or host birthday parties. Competitive climbing was only a few years old, and there were just a handful of competitive climbers in the world."

Though climbing gyms have proliferated in recent decades, the conceit of artificial climbing structures is not a new idea. The first known structure designed for teaching and practicing rock climbing was Monitor Rock, a masonry project erected at the edge of a golf course in West Seattle, Washington, in 1938, championed by Clark Schurman. Roughly twenty-eight feet tall, the edifice—now known as Schurman Rock—included a slab, chimneys, and overhangings, as well as a concrete "glacier," and hosted many of the day's greatest climbers, including Fred Beckey. The first indoor climbing wall is believed to have been erected at the Ullswater School in Penrith, England, using bricks and stone for hand- and footholds. It was not until 1987 that the first climbing gym opened in the States, fittingly enough, in Seattle. Vertical World is still in operation today.

OPPOSITE:

Kletterzentrum
Innsbruck
showcases
the fantastic
possibilities of
climbing gyms.

Times certainly have changed. As of 2018, more than 450 climbing and bouldering gyms are operating in North America; Germany and Japan each have nearly that many. Francis shared his thoughts on the explosive growth of indoor climbing facilities: "Early on, you didn't find climbing gyms in places where there was no outdoor climbing. Conventional wisdom was that the gyms couldn't survive. Now you can go into the heart of the city and find climbing gyms. By the late '90s, climbing gyms began drawing the fitness crowd—people who were going to Gold's Gym and 24 Hour Fitness. They were social places where you could meet girls and guys, and learn a new skill too. Climbing gyms came to be seen as a good place to hang out and get fit in an encouraging environment.

"Climbing gyms have also become an important place for a new generation of climbers to be exposed to the sport. There are no falling rocks, so you don't have to worry about helmets and other safety concerns. It's a controlled playground where kids can get focused on the sport. It's the young climbers who grew up in gyms that are really pushing the limits of rock climbing out in the field. Most of today's elite climbers have a competitive gym background."

For competitive and casual climbers alike, Kletterzentrum Innsbruck holds great promise. Constructed in partnership with the City of Innsbruck, the State of Tyrol, and the Innsbruck Alpine Association, the gym boasts over sixty-five thousand square feet of climbing surface, split between lead, boulder, and speed climbing. Kletterzentrum Innsbruck opened its doors in May 2017; open to the public, it also serves as the training and competition center for the Austrian National Climbing Team.

"I think that Kletterzentrum Innsbruck is super aspirational for what climbing is going to be," Francis opined. "They're trying to create a European climbing hub, and they see the gym's potential to boost climbing tourism. It begins with its exterior, with angular white walls—its striking modernist architecture. Inside it's so expansive, it would take you a week to climb on all the angles and surfaces. The care they've taken in their route setting takes the climbing gym to the next level. There's an entire system of checks and balances to maintain the quality of the climbing routes. They take it seriously." For what it's worth, Kletterzentrum Innsbruck also has a beautiful café that serves up excellent cappuccinos, among other treats.

Climbing gyms once sought to emulate the rocks walls encountered in nature. In the future, this could be quite different. "I think that you'll see climbing being integrated more and more into urban environments," Francis said. "The gyms are breaking ties with the outdoor environment, where they took their original inspiration. Some of the biggest design statements are with the walls themselves; some in Japan glow in the dark. They're becoming giant sculptures.

"Gyms are also becoming much more diverse. There's a place in Memphis called Memphis Rox. Membership is free; the gym asks for donations. Kids are climbing for free, hanging out, doing their homework. It's gym as community center—a pretty cool model for what a climbing gym can do for a community."

FRANCIS SANZARO, PhD, is editor of *Rock and Ice, Ascent,* and *Gym Climber* magazines. He completed his doctorate in philosophy of religion at Syracuse University in 2012 and is the author of several books, including *The Boulder: A Philosophy for Bouldering; The Infantile Grotesque: Pathology, Sexuality and a Theory of Religion;* and *Society Elsewhere: Why the Gravest Threat to Humanity Will Come from Within.* Francis lives in the mountains of Colorado with his wife and two children, and is generally either climbing, writing, or philosophizing. Learn about his latest projects at www.fsanzaro.com.

If You Go

► **Getting There:** Innsbruck is served by a number of carriers from cities across Europe, including London, Vienna, and Amsterdam.
► **Best Time to Visit**: Kletterzentrum Innsbruck (+43 512397340; www.kletter zentrum-innsbruck.at) is open year-round, though is subject to occasional closures for competitions/Austrian national team training.
► **Level of Difficulty**: There's something for everyone at Kletterzentrum Innsbruck.
► **Accommodations**: Innsbruck Tourismus (+43 51253560; www.innsbruck.info) highlights lodging options in and around the city.

THE BUGABOOS

RECOMMENDED BY **Kolin Powick**

It's safe to say that the Bugaboos have made a strong impression on Kolin Powick. "I still get chills when I say it," he began. "It's a super-special place for me. Part of it is the climbing, but there are many other reasons. My wife and I are both from Calgary, which is relatively close to the Bugaboos, so I'd heard about it for a long time. I'm more of a trad and alpine climber; my wife is more of a sport climber. When we were dating, she'd take me to places to clip bolts, and I'd take her to trad routes in the Canadian Rockies and alpine and mountaineering adventures in Alaska. Pretty early on in our relationship, we went to the Bugaboos. Honestly, it wasn't the best trip. We didn't have great weather, and we weren't able to get up the routes we wanted—particularly, the Beckey-Chouinard on South Howser Tower. But still, it was beautiful—my kind of scene.

"Fast-forward ten years. Ellen and I got married, went on a one-year North American climbing honeymoon, and became better climbers. All our free time was spent climbing, and we were fortunate enough to be able to climb all over the world. We were living in Salt Lake City and had demanding jobs. At this point in our lives, time for extended climbing trips was precious. We've always been big dog people and within a matter of twelve months, both of our dogs passed away—it hit us pretty hard. In order to decompress and without the worry of having to find someone to look after 'the boys,' we decided it was a good time to head back to 'the Bugs' and see if we could realize that earlier goal of climbing Beckey-Chouinard."

Bugaboo Provincial Park rests in the Purcell Mountains of southeastern British Columbia. If climbers were asked to craft an ideal alpine playground, this is what they would likely have come up with: a vast collection of granite spires in a panoply of shapes, all framed by endless vistas of mountains and glaciers. The tallest spire, the North Tower

OPPOSITE:
The granite spires of the Bugaboos provide an alpine playground and are home to one of North America's greatest routes, Beckey-Chouinard.

7

DESTINATION

at Howser Spire, eclipses eleven thousand feet. Topher Donahue described the surreal terrain this way in his book, *Bugaboo Dreams*: "In the surrounding mountains, the glaciers shaped the softer sedimentary rocks as well, but left more rugged faces as if the carving force of the glacier were in the hands of a drunk with a bulldozer." (The Bugaboos, incidentally, take their name from a failed gold prospecting expedition in the late 1890s; a "bugaboo" was a miner's term for a dead end.) Though prospectors came up empty here, climbers soon found great riches in the area. Early efforts were led by Conrad Kain, a renowned Austrian climber who, beginning in the second decade of the 1900s, went on to put up more than sixty first ascents in western Canada, including on Bugaboo Spire and Mount Robson in Banff National Park. By the late 1950s, another generation of climbers, including Fred Beckey and Yvon Chouinard, had discovered the possibilities of the Bugaboos. Their activities here included the establishment of the route on the South Tower of the Howser Spire Massif, which today bears their name: a 15-pitch, 5.10 climb that spans two thousand feet on a large buttress, with fantastic views thrown in for good measure.

Most of the climbers who make their way to the South Tower will experience a fairly grueling hike of eight to ten hours, part of it across Vowell Glacier—perhaps with an overnight along the way at the Kain Hut or Applebee Dome. (Climbers who camp there should be sure to encircle their vehicles with chicken wire to discourage porcupines from snacking on the tires and tubing; scientists believe they're drawn to cars for the salt, not the taste of rubber.) Due to time constraints, Kolin and Ellen decided to fly in by helicopter. "We flew to Calgary, borrowed the in-laws' car, and drove to Bugaboo Lodge. We'd arranged a helicopter through Canadian Mountain Holidays to take us in to East Creek, which is ideally situated for an approach to Beckey-Chouinard—and outside of the park, which doesn't allow helicopters to land. The pilot did a fly-by of the route before landing—it looked incredible—and we were stoked. We landed on the glacier, right below the line, complete with coolers with steaks, wine, and beer—we were living large. That night, I asked Ellen if she wanted to do some warm-up climbs to get our granite game on, or just go for it. The forecast was perfect—she wanted to go for it.

"We woke up the next morning to a bluebird day, having the whole place to ourselves. It was an easy approach, a ten-minute downhill sneaker run to the line. The weather was perfect; we climbed in lightweight shells and shared a single light puffy at the belays. For some reason, and quite surprisingly, I was actually climbing well that day, as was Ellen—

though she always does! Generally, I am conservative and like to go slow and steady, but that day I was climbing with confidence. I hadn't climbed on alpine granite for quite some time, and found the friction of the coarse rock a welcome relief to the glacier-polished granite of Little Cottonwood Canyon in Salt Lake City that I had been climbing on recently. The route isn't particularly hard—mostly 5.8s and 5.9s, with a few pitches of 5.10. We swung leads the entire way and were lucky enough to be the only party on the route. We had fired a dream route of mine the first day of our trip, and by the time we rappelled down, we were joking 'We're done! We can go home now.' We hadn't even been in camp for twenty-four hours."

As it turned out, Kolin and Ellen *didn't* end up going home after sending Beckey-Chouinard. "Any time I'm hanging out with my wife is a good time, and in the mountains, it's just that much better. It was so great to be able to unplug for a time, reflect on the loss of our dogs, and enjoy the pristine alpine setting and incredible climbing of the Bugaboos. We had the East Creek camp to ourselves for a full week, had splitter weather the entire time, and ended up being so exhausted from all the walking and climbing that we were almost hoping for bad weather to force a rest day, but it never came. At the end of the week, we had tallied six different routes on six different spires, having started our week off with the route I'd always dreamed of—the Beckey-Chouinard.

"It was total heaven."

KOLIN POWICK is a Canadian ex-pat who moved to Salt Lake City with his wife, Ellen, more than twenty years ago for the access to climbing. Currently a mechanical engineer, Kolin was the Director of Quality at Black Diamond Equipment for more than eleven years and has been the Climbing Category Director at Black Diamond Equipment since 2014. His climbing travels have taken him all over the world, where he's always happy to have his strong wife put up the rope.

If You Go

▶ **Getting There:** Domestic flights on Air Canada (888-247-2262; www.aircanada.com) serve Cranbrook, which is roughly 150 miles from the provincial park parking area.

Calgary, roughly two hundred miles away, is served by many major carriers. Should you opt for a helicopter ride in, contact Canadian Mountain Holidays (800-661-0252; www.cmhheli.com).

► **Best Time to Visit**: The climbing season is June to September, with July and August having the best chance of good weather.

► **Level of Difficulty**: Though many climbs are tall, there are routes in the 5.4 to 5.8 that will be accessible for climbers of moderate ability.

► **Guides**: Several guidebooks are available, including *The Bugaboos: One of the World's Great Alpine Rockclimbing Centres* (Chris Atkinson and Marc Piche). A number of guide services lead climbers in the area.

► **Accommodations**: There are several camping options: the Conrad Kain hut (www.alpine clubofcanada.ca) has the most amenities; you should book in advance. Applebee Dome is forty-five minutes farther up the trail, but cheaper. Wilderness camping is available at East Springs, which is just outside of the provincial park.

SQUAMISH

RECOMMENDED BY **Katy Holm**

When the gorges of the East Coast and the canyon country of the Southwest become too humid or hot to climb comfortably, many look north and west to British Columbia and the granite walls of Squamish.

"Squamish is a world-class granite destination," Katy Holm began. "We're fortunate to have some of the highest-quality rock around. Historically, it has been trad climbing that brings people to Squamish. There's solid rock to satisfy a broad range of abilities, and plenty of quality climbs from 5.7 to 5.13 and beyond. There's a reason some of the best climbers in the world show up here in the summer months—though there's a lot for people starting crack climbing too. In recent years, bouldering has really blown up around Squamish. And there's some fine sport climbing too. Another special thing about the region as a climbing destination is the town itself. Squamish is a place where people enjoy hanging out in the summer. There are tons of bakeries, breweries, coffee shops, and other nice amenities. Though people have been coming here for outdoor sports recreation for a while—Squamish is also known for its kitesurfing, windsurfing, and mountain biking—it's still not that touristy. Part of the attraction is it doesn't have the glitz of a place like Whistler."

Squamish rests on the western edge of the province of British Columbia, midway between the city of Vancouver and the aforementioned ski mecca of Whistler. Tucked against the northeastern edge of Howe Sound, the town takes its name from the Squamish Nation, a First Nations people that historically inhabited the southern coast of the province. From a climber's perspective, Squamish first and foremost means Stawamus Chief—or simply, the Chief—a granitic monolith that looms nearly 2,300 feet above the town and the sound. The first known ascents on the Chief were recorded in the late

1950s, which is when the first highway from Vancouver opened up, thus initiating Squamish's slow transformation from lumber town to outdoor destination. (That stretch of highway—now known as the Sea to Sky corridor—is considered one of North America's most scenic coastal drives.) The first ascents of one of the Chief's main attractions, the Grand Wall, were achieved by Ed Cooper and Jim Baldwin in 1961. Since then, more than three hundred routes have been identified on the Chief . . . though it's certainly not the only game in town.

"For beginning climbers, I love an area called the Smoke Bluffs," Katy continued. "It's a little zone of crags that are dotted throughout a forested hillside. There are hundreds and hundreds of single-pitch climbs that can be top-roped or lead-climbed, overlooking the sound. You can find your own little zone in there, and it's a pretty area—a little wonderland. Climbers of greater skill can progress to Shlanay [known to some as the Squaw], another great chunk of granite. Shlanay has lots of high-quality five-pitch climbs, perfect for half-day excursions. One ascent I like there is Jungle Warfare [5.10a]. One of my favorites is the Great Game [four-hundred-foot elevation, 5.10c/d]. There are some bolted anchors near the top now, though when I first did it, there weren't any. You had to follow the weaknesses in the monolith and manage your gear right so you didn't get to the top and find yourself with nothing left. The sense of adventure was great."

More advanced climbers—or strong intermediates with a stomach for exposure—will next make their way to the Chief and Squamish's most celebrated route, the Grand Wall (5.11a). As the Mountain Project website has noted, this ascent "has it all: perfect rock, great setting, runout slab, stellar crack, strenuous laybacking, delicate face, and many variations." As Katy puts it, "The Grand Wall goes right up the heart of the Chief. It's really a classic. The quality of the rock for every pitch [generally nine as you gain a thousand feet] is incredible, and there's great diversity of climbing and movement to reach the top. When you look over your shoulder, you see the Sound backed by mountains. I have some fine memories of that climb, the feeling of moving over the granite, the warmth of the early evening sun when you're on the top, sore and satisfied, the view over Howe Sound as the sun begins to set. If you want more punishment, you can tackle University Wall [5.12], another classic that's a test piece for the best climbers."

A lot of route development is happening in Squamish with many beginner to advanced routes developed each year. If you want to get away from the crowds, newer areas are a good idea. Free topos of newer routes can be found on Quickdraw Publications' website

OPPOSITE: Kristie Lonczak on Perry's Lieback, a 5.11a on Squamish's most famous wall, the Grand Wall.

and the Squamish Rock Guides' blog. Or come into Climb On, the local climbing store, and ask the staff for ideas. If you are in Climb On, consider donating to the bolt fund, which supports local route development. When you combine the three hundred-plus routes on the Chief with the Climbs at Shlanay, Smoke Bluffs, and other venues, there are over 1,200 rock climbing routes in the Squamish area—not to mention double that number of bouldering problems, many near the base of the Grand Wall.

Part of the appeal of climbing around Squamish is enjoying the total experience of Squamish. Katy described how she might entertain a visiting climber. "I'd start the day with a nice cup of coffee at one of the coffee shops we have in town. Counterpart Coffee and 1914 are two good ones, and Tall Tree Bakery has great pastries. Since most of the bigger climbs are between five and fifteen pitches, and the summer days are long, you don't need to get going at five A.M. to get your climbing in. You can enjoy a leisurely coffee, do a world-class climb, and have a nice meal afterward. If you've got the skills, you should definitely tackle the Grand Wall. I'd also recommend a day of bouldering. And the Pet Wall—short for 'petrifying'—offers some fine granite sport climbing. I'd also leave a day to visit one or our beautiful mountain lakes. As for dinner, Essence of India, Saha Lebanese food, several sushi restaurants, and the Coppercoil Grill are just a few of a number of good places to eat. If drinks is what you are after, there are two local breweries, Back Country and A-Frame, and a few cideries in town, which also serve delicious food. For dinner with a view, consider Watershed Grill, which is right on the Squamish River. There might be seals in the river, and you're looking up at the Tantalus Range. And there are festivals going all summer long, with live music."

KATY HOLM began climbing as a twelve-year-old girl when her whole family took a guided rock course at Fleming Beach bouldering area in Victoria, British Columbia. From that moment on, she knew she needed rock climbing in her life. Katy is an accomplished alpine and rock climber who has gone on many international expeditions, and is a co-owner of Climb On Squamish (climbonsquamish.com). Before Climb On, she spent ten years working for Mountain Equipment Co-op. These days Katy can be found projecting hard trad lines with her husband, Kelly, or teaching her daughter, Ruby, to climb at the Smoke Bluffs. She loves sea kayaking, skiing, and gardening.

If You Go

▶ **Getting There:** Squamish is roughly an hour from Vancouver, which is served by most major carriers.

▶ **Best Time to Visit**: The drier summer months attract most of Squamish's climbing visitors.

▶ **Level of Difficulty**: With more than 1,200 climbs, Squamish offers something for everyone, though climbers hoping to tackle the bigger ascents on the Chief should have at least intermediate climbing skills.

▶ **Guides**: There are a number of guiding services around Squamish, including Squamish Rock Guides (604-892-7816; www.squamishrockguides.com). Several guide-books are also available, including *Squamish Select* (Marc Bourdon) and *The Climbers Guide to Squamish* (Kevin McLane).

▶ **Accommodations**: There are many camping opportunities around Squamish, includ-ing Stawamus Chief Provincial Park Campground right at the Chief. Camping and other options are highlighted at Tourism Squamish (www.exploresquamish.com).

BISHOP

RECOMMENDED BY **Jeff Deikis**

California's most concentrated assemblage of sport climbing routes, some of the world's best bouldering, and a stunning landscape to boot: For those with a vertical inclination, you might say that Bishop has an embarrassment of riches.

"When I moved to Bishop from the Midwest, I was as attracted by the world-class bouldering as I was the skiing," Jeff Deikis began. "Mammoth, one of California's largest ski resorts, lies just forty miles north of the High Sierra and offers endless backcountry pursuits. The two major bouldering areas near town, the Buttermilks and the Volcanic Tablelands, are famous around the world for their quality, height, and abundance. For roped climbing in the winter, the Owens River Gorge is just up the road and offers more than a thousand sport climbing options. When temps get hotter, just head to Pine Creek Canyon, where, in the last few years, there's been a wealth of development. Of course, you also have the Sierra Nevada mountains to explore and plug gear in—exquisite alpine granite at thirteen thousand feet.

"And, honestly, the landscape is just amazing. Bishop is located four thousand feet in the high desert, nestled on a valley floor between the White Mountains, which rise fourteen thousand feet to the immediate east, and the stunning Eastern Sierra Nevada, which rise fourteen thousand feet to the west. There are no foothills—just sudden, craggy peaks. And while Mammoth gets six hundred inches of snow a year, it's not necessary to even own a snow shovel when living in Bishop."

When it comes to the rocks, the 325-acre Buttermilk Country is at the top of the list. "The Buttermilks sit right at the foot of the Sierra," Jeff continued. "The mountains are right there, and you have dramatic views of both the surrounding ranges and the vast Owens Valley, spilling out below. Many of the boulders are juggernauts—some stand as

OPPOSITE:
Tim Leary
appreciates some
"buttermilking"
in the dramatic
325-acre
Buttermilk
Country
near Bishop.

large as a two-story house—though many others are more modestly sized. They are granite, but heavily featured with holds of all shapes and sizes." Bouldering around the Buttermilks—"Buttermilking" in local parlance—dates back to the early 1940s, when Smoke Blanchard began assembling a series of problems that came to be known as Smoke's Rock Course. Smoke's son Bob continued in his father's trailblazing work. Jeff described a few noteworthy climbs. "Grandma Peabody is one of the defining boulders. It's forty-plus feet tall—not for the faint of heart. But there are many ways up, from V0 to V12. Ironman Traverse [V4, on Iron Man Boulder] is another rock that's always on visitors' tick lists. Grandpa Peabody Boulder has several classic test pieces that go up the steepest face of the rock—Evilution to the Lip is V10, Evilution, if you pull the lip, is V12 or 13. Another is the Mandala [V12, on Mandala/Pope's Prow Boulder], which was put up by Chris Sharma in 2000.

"Down at a lower elevation you can find the Volcanic Tablelands. Here, the boulders consist of volcanic tuff. The boulders here are divided into two main areas—the Happies, which were developed in the '80s, and the Sads, which were developed in the '90s. The boulders here have more overhanging rock and are generally less tall than the Buttermilks, with juggier, more positive holds. One favorite here is the Hulk in the Happies, a V6 that Peter Croft put up. Both the Tablelands and the Buttermilks are world class on their own. Having them both so close is a gift. As a local, if it's warmer weather we'll go to the Buttermilks; if it's cooler out, we'll head to the Happies and Sads."

Of course, many will visit greater Bishop and never set foot (or hand) on a boulder. For those folks, it's all about sport climbing. "The routes in the Owens River Gorge are amazing—vertical to slightly hanging, with pumpy, open handholds. The routes are longer than typical," Jeff said. "Many are over thirty meters. Since there are plenty of routes on each side of the river, you can usually find sun or shade. It's a great training zone, as you can get in a lot of vertical feet in a day. When it begins to get too hot to climb in the Gorge, climbers head to Pine Creek Canyon, which is at a higher elevation. One popular crag there—the Mustache Wall—has vertical to overhanging granite with bolted, single-pitch routes—while many others are multi-pitch trad or mixed. Pratt's Crack [5.9] is a great offwidth test piece at Scheelite Canyon, put up by Chuck Pratt. It's burly."

When you come off the rocks, the town of Bishop has you covered in terms of sustenance. "There are a few coffee shops in town," Jeff described, "all of which will cover you for your caffeine fix, though the Black Sheep is the official local climber hangout, and it's near Eastside Sports, which has climbing supplies. There's a famous bakery called Schats, but Great Basin Bakery is the local beta on scoring good bagels, pastries, and breakfast sandwiches. Mountain Rambler Brewery has the best local beer and food too." It's also worth noting that there are a number of hot springs between Bishop and Mammoth— some that can be visited for a fee, and some that are less formal, and free.

JEFF DEIKIS serves as American Alpine Club's creative director, overseeing content development, graphic design, and brand management. Originally from Ann Arbor, Michigan, but introduced to the outdoors before he could walk, he is an avid climber and backcountry snowboarder with some thirty-plus years of mountain experience. Jeff has been working within the outdoor industry for more than fourteen years, in various marketing and program-development roles. He is also an award-winning photographer and avid world traveler. Jeff can usually be found milling around the Eastern Sierra, his trusty pooch, Obi, in tow.

If You Go

► **Getting There:** The nearest commercial airport is thirty-five miles from Bishop in Mammoth Lakes, which is served by United (800-864-8331; www.united.com) and, seasonally, Alaska (800-252-7522; www.alaskaair.com). Reno, Nevada, which is served by more carriers, is roughly four hours away.

► **Best Time to Visit**: There's four-season bouldering/climbing around Bishop, depending on where you go. Buttermilk is more comfortable during warmer times; Tablelands when it's colder.

► **Level of Difficulty**: There's an incredible variety of options for climbers of all levels, between Bishop, Owens River Gorge, and Pine Creek Canyon.

► **Guides**: A number of good guides are available, including *Bishop Bouldering* (Wills Young) and *Bishop Area Rock Climbs* (Peter Croft and Marty Lewis). Sierra Mountain Guides (760-648-1122; www.sierramtnguides.com) leads climbs in the area.

► **Accommodations**: Bishop Visitor Center (760-873-8405; www.bishopvisitor.com) highlights both camping and motel options in the region.

JOSHUA TREE NATIONAL PARK

RECOMMENDED BY **Leslie Timms**

"There's something about the energy of Joshua Tree that pulls me in," Leslie Timms reflected. "The second I'm there, the rest of the world doesn't exist. Joshua Tree seems like it's been dropped from another planet—the vibe, the scenery, and the climbing. The grades are hard, the climbing is bold, and there's such a rich history. Even though it's one of the most visited climbing venues around, it feels very adventurous. There's always a place you can wander to and be on your own. A life's worth of climbing awaits. I'm the worst climber I can be when I'm there—it scares and humbles me that much. But at the same time, it's a healing place—it puts things in perspective and grounds me. The feeling Joshua Tree gives off is unexplainable, and not everyone feels it. But for those who have that connection, the park is unlike anywhere else."

Joshua Tree National Park spans nearly eight hundred thousand acres in southern California, roughly 140 miles east of Los Angeles. The park's eponymous tree, which is a member of the agave family, received its name from Mormon settlers, who were reminded of the biblical figure Joshua by the tree's limbs, which seemed to be out-stretched in supplication. The high desert monzogranite of the Joshua Tree region once provided shelter in wintertime for Native American peoples. By the 1940s, it had been discovered by the Sierra Club's Rock Climbing Section; by the 1950s, climbing pioneers like Royal Robbins and Mark Powell began exploring the seemingly endless opportunities available—more than eight thousand climbing routes and two thousand bouldering problems to date.

"At Joshua Tree, it's as if a bunch of granite dinosaur eggs were dropped in the desert," Leslie continued. "The formations are almost like rock sculptures. They take on different colors as the sun dances across the sky, casting shadows of different shapes. My first visit

OPPOSITE:
Rob Moellering
nears the top
of Lost Pencil
on Weasel Boys
Arete, a 5.12b
test piece.

57

was part of my first-ever climbing trip. I came out of the climbing gym in Canada and did a U.S. tour with friends. We arrived at Hidden Valley, which is the hub of climbing at Joshua Tree. There's a crazy energy there—L.A. hippies running around, dirtbag climbers from all over. Some seem to have been there for ages. We were sport climbers and boulderers at the time, of moderate skill. We got out on this 5.10 sport climb, and absolutely crapped our pants. We barely got to the top, almost in tears, and we didn't know how to get down. But still we wanted to stay. Every year we'd go back, and get better and better. The climbs aren't all that tall; you might be only sixty feet up, but you feel like you're on the top of the world. Visiting Joshua Tree encouraged us to build the tools in our toolbox, and opened our eyes to real rock climbing."

Leslie likes to warm up with some bouldering before tackling wall ascents. "There are some awesome circuits," she said. "If you find the right circuits, you can go with your pad and experience some classic boulder problems. For me, it's a dress rehearsal, a chance to remember the style of the cracks and practice for the big stuff." For Leslie, the "big stuff" means Acid Crack, a classic 5.12 trad route on a high Southwest Face in the Real Hidden Valley. "John Bachar put that climb up in 1982," she continued. "It was always a dream of mine to send that route. The day I first did it, I went with no expectations. I let go of everything and it all came together. When I summited, I had an out-of-this-world experience. I felt like Bachar was there with me. With Acid Crack done, I felt like I'd graduated to a new level. One of my fantasies was to be a Stone Master like John Bachar. Conquering Acid Crack was a big step in that direction."

For many, the opportunity to hang out at Hidden Valley Campground is an essential part of the pilgrimage. "There are lots of fun little adventures you can have in the campground, and all the most famous climbing spots are in walking distance," Leslie enthused. "It's often full, you almost need to stalk it. And you've got to be there before the weekend." There's not much in the way of services around the park. For groceries, Leslie recommends heading to 29 Palms or Yucca Valley; for a meal out or a laundry stop, visit the town of Joshua Tree. "The best coffee place ever is there—Joshua Tree Coffee Company," she added.

Leslie's first successful summit of Acid Crack will always remain with her. But one of her more modest ascents also captures that elusive Joshua Tree vibe. "At Hidden Valley, there's a little free solo climb up to a spot we call the Space Station," she recalled. "It's a giant hole in the rock and there's room for people to sit and take in the scenery. I remember one season being up in the Space Station watching the sunset. It was perfectly aligned. As the sun was setting, a bluegrass band [that was staying in the campground] began to play. We just sat up there, as the band played, watching the stars beginning to emerge."

LESLIE TIMMS is a professional rock guide and owner of On the Rocks Climbing Guides (www.ontherocksclimbing.com) in Thornbury, Ontario. She spends April through October each year running a successful climbing guiding company and teaching PCGI guide certification courses across Ontario (www.climbingguidesinstitute.org). Her days off from guiding are spent climbing and developing new routes along the Niagara Escarpment. During the Canadian winter months, Leslie and her husband hit the road with their thirteen-foot trailer, "Trilly," to chase sun and climb rocks across the United States and the globe. Her most memorable ascent was getting the first ascent (FA) of the most difficult traditional/mixed route at Lions Head, Ontario: Above the Clouds (5.13b). Leslie is a fixture in the Ontario climbing community and continues to push herself to new levels in the sport, year after year.

If You Go

▶ **Getting There:** The closest airport to Joshua Tree is in Palm Springs, which is served by several carriers, including Alaska (800-252-7522; www.alaskaair.com) and United (800-864-8331; www.united.com). Los Angeles is about 140 miles west.

▶ **Best Time to Visit**: Mid-October to mid-May is prime time, when cooler temperatures grace the desert.

▶ **Level of Difficulty**: There are a tremendous variety of climbing options in Joshua Tree, from entry-level bouldering to 5.12+++.

▶ **Guides**: A number of guide services lead excursions in Joshua Tree. The National Park Service lists authorized guides at www.nps.gov/jotr/.

▶ **Accommodations**: There are eight campgrounds in Joshua Tree National Park; four (including Hidden Valley) are on a first-come/first-served basis. Modest motels are available in the towns of 29 Palms and Joshua Tree.

YOSEMITE NATIONAL PARK

RECOMMENDED BY **Kevin Jorgeson**

Reaching the age of sixteen is a milestone for many American teens, the chance to pursue the freedom of the open road . . . assuming you can pass your state driving test and have access to a car. For Kevin Jorgeson, his sixteenth birthday signaled a freedom of a vertical nature. "When I turned sixteen, my dad took me to Yosemite," he recalled. "I'd been doing a lot of climbing and was beginning to compete, and he thought it was time. I remember getting there and being so inspired. It became a ritual to go every birthday. This led to more and more time there. At first, I was bouldering for the most part when we'd visit. But my climbing didn't take little steps—it advanced by leaps and bounds. I went from boulders to big walls."

Fast-forward to 2009. "I had just finished a big bouldering project and was looking for something new, a new discipline," Kevin continued. "That's when I saw a video clip of Tommy Caldwell working on a crazy El Capitan project. I asked if he needed a partner."

Yosemite National Park comprises 1,160 square miles of mostly wilderness terrain, flowing across the west flank of the Sierra Nevadas.

From a rock climbing perspective, it's hard to overemphasize Yosemite's significance. MountainProject.com puts it quite well:

> Yosemite Valley is THE PLACE for many rock climbers. A literal mecca for climbers across the globe, the crags and walls of "The Valley" see thousands of climber-days in the course of a year. During the height of the season, it's typical to hear climbers on El Capitan yelling back and forth in English, German, Japanese, Russian, and many other languages. In this one place, many factors come together to form a nearly perfect arena for rock climbing: mild weather, beautiful scenery, and incredible granite walls perfectly suited to climbing.

OPPOSITE:
Jim Herson
tackles
Salathe Wall
on Yosemite's
infamous
El Capitan.

Yosemite's role in the history of American rock climbing is as pronounced as its vaulted position on every climber's bucket list. One of the most colorful periods came in the 1950s, when two climbing legends—Royal Robbins and Warren Harding—were engaged in a casual competition for first ascents in Yosemite. Harding had set his sights on Half Dome, the iconic granite edifice that rises 4,737 feet from the east end of the valley. But in July 1957, Robbins, accompanied by Mike Sherrick and Jerry Gallwas, made the climb over the course of five days on what's come to be known as the Regular Northwest Face. Harding soon pledged that he'd go for adjacent El Capitan—at the time, the greatest prize in rock climbing. In the spring of 1958, Harding and his team began their ascent, via the route that's known as the Nose. The climb was done in stages over weekends, and required that the team develop new methods and equipment—including the chest harness. Progress was painfully slow, but after forty-five days of climbing, Harding, George Whitmore, and Wayne Merry reached the top.

The project Tommy Caldwell was considering in 2009 was a free climb (with ropes for protection only) of the Dawn Wall on El Cap's southeast face—the steepest and blankest section of the wall . . . and at 5.14d, considered by many to be the most difficult big-wall free climb in the world. For the next six years, Tommy and Kevin spent hundreds of days piecing together the path that would take them to the top. On December 27, 2014, they began their ascent. For the next nineteen days, they made their way to the top over thirty-two pitches, with a support team providing supplies to their portaledge base camp. Along the way, filmmakers were present to capture the moment. The resulting film, *The Dawn Wall*, was released in September 2018, bringing international attention to the valley and the sport of rock climbing.

Though another climbing film concerning Yosemite (Alex Honnold's *Free Solo*) may have stolen some of the thunder of *The Dawn Wall*, Kevin and Tommy's accomplishment on El Cap remains an incredible climbing milestone. "Topping out on the Dawn Wall is a memory that I won't soon forget," Kevin shared. "It was the culmination of a six- or seven-year dream. But I can still have fun over in Yosemite. There are more fun days than big stressful days. The best way to experience the park as a climber is to follow in the footsteps of the classics."

KEVIN JORGESON is widely recognized as one of the best big-wall rock climbers in the world, and is well known for being able to free climb sheer cliffs and high ball large boulders.

He grew up in Santa Rosa, California, spending time in the outdoors with his dad, hiking, white-water rafting, fishing, hunting, and camping. At age ten, he discovered the sport of rock climbing and never looked back. By age seventeen, he was an International Champion. After a seven-year quest to find a way to free climb the steepest, blankest face of Yosemite's monolithic El Capitan, Kevin and Tommy Caldwell finally stood atop the Dawn Wall with the world watching. Even President Barack Obama was moved by their nineteen-day climb, stating, "You remind us that anything is possible." In addition to his climbing achievements, Kevin has spearheaded 1Climb (www.1climb.org), an initiative to introduce children to climbing, which includes a partnership with Boys & Girls Clubs of America to build climbing walls in their club facilities. He is a much sought-after speaker and an entrepreneur, having launched Session (www.sessionclimbing.com), a world-class climbing facility in Sonoma County, California. Learn more about Kevin at www.kevinjorgeson.com.

If You Go

► **Getting There:** The Fresno-Yosemite International Airport is roughly 2.5 hours to Yosemite Valley and is served by many airlines, including Alaska (800-252-7522; www.alaskaair.com) and American (800-433-7300; www.aa.com). Yosemite is approximately four hours from Bay Area airports.

► **Best Time to Visit**: Climbing conditions are best in spring (mid-March through June) and early fall (September through October).

► **Level of Difficulty**: Most routes in Yosemite begin around 5.8 and escalate from there.

► **Guides**: There are a number of guidebooks available, including *Yosemite Valley Free Climbs: Supertopos* (Chris McNamara, Steve Roper, Todd Snyder, and Greg Barnes) and *Yosemite Bigwalls: The Complete Guide* (Roger Putnam and Erik Sloan). Several guides lead climbs in Yosemite, including Yosemite Mountaineering School & Guide Service (209-372-8344; www.travelyosemite.com).

► **Accommodations**: Yosemite has thirteen campgrounds; seven are served by a reservation system, the others are first-come/first-served. Visit www.nps.gov/yose for an overview of sites; visit www.recreation.gov or call 877-444-6777 for reservations.

LIMING

RECOMMENDED BY **Michael Dobie**

It was the confluence of several ambitions that brought Michael Dobie to Liming. "It was back in 2008 that I began to get serious about climbing," he recalled. "I also had ambitions to leave the United States and see the world. Around that time, I was introduced to the idea of developing new climbing routes as a way to serve the climbing community. In 2010, I had the opportunity to go to Yangshuo to test out a career change from athletic training to outdoor education/rock climbing. Yangshuo is popular for its limestone climbing, but people there were talking about other possibilities in Yunnan Province.

"A climbing friend, Austin Stringham, moved to the Lijiang region in Yunnan to set up a climbing operation there, and invited me to help him out. We looked at a number of places, including Liming. There was wonderful sandstone with lots of cracks. We went to the local officials to get permission to rock climb in the area. It was a long process. My friend's girlfriend, Laojiu, helped us translate a proposal outlining how we'd develop the area for trad climbing. We were given the go-ahead. My friend's company didn't work out, but I stayed on. I'd invite other climbing friends to come and help me develop routes. Some North Face climbers came in 2011, and that got Liming some media attention. In 2012, North Face China pledged to support me to continue developing climbing in the area. Before Liming, trad climbing didn't really exist in China."

Liming sits in the mountainous northwestern corner of Yunnan Province, which rests in the southwestern corner of China. Liming rests at an elevation of seven thousand feet, and some of the climbing crags sit at heights greater than nine thousand feet; Jade Dragon Snow Mountain, for example, which is 18,360 feet, is in the vicinity. Though recreational climbing is very new to the mountains of Liming, local people have been scaling the cliffs with long wooden ladders for hundreds of years to harvest honey from bees' nests in the rocks.

OPPOSITE:
Logan Barber
takes on Firewall,
a 5.13d that is
considered one of
the two hardest
trad routes in
China (and has
been climbed
by only a few
others).

"The area around Liming is very wooded, with pine trees among the red sandstone," Mike continued. "Some people liken it to Indian Creek at Moab. While the climbing has a similar style—lots of crack climbs—the overall feeling of the place is more a rainforest or jungle than a desert. To date, we've established more than 350 trad climbs. I feel like the good stuff starts at the 5.9 level. The Great Owl is crack climbing 101 for those who haven't done much crack climbing. Right next door is a nice 5.10, Scarface 2, as it resembles Scarface at Indian Creek. The best 5.10 might be Wind of the Valley, a hand-crack corner that's about 100 feet. The Feedbag is also up there. It's 125 feet, quite varied, starting with a chimneyish climb, then a splitter crack and finally some face climbing. Japanese Pixelated Genitals is also popular. At the end there's a roof traverse with nothing but air beneath you. It's reminiscent of Kachoong, a popular route at Arapiles in Australia. For more advanced climbers, I like Back to Primitive [5.11, 8 pitches]. Japanese Cowboy [5.12] is a great crack climb. An area called Guardian has some nice 5.11s and bolted 5.12s. If you really want a challenge, there are a few 5.13s—Firewall and the Honeycomb Dome.

"I left for a few years but came back in 2018. I was getting more into sport climbing. Chinese climbers are more acquainted with sport climbing. I realized that putting up some bolts in Liming would be a great way to attract sport climbers to the area and then try to introduce them to trad climbing. We've now added seventy or so sport climbs. This gives the area a broader appeal and makes it more well-rounded."

Most climbers will stay at the Faraway Hotel, which is a convenient distance to the crags. "It's run by a local family," Mike continued, "and I've been working with them to better accommodate Western visitors and climbers. [Most of the people here are from the Lisu ethnic group; through most of China the Han are the dominant ethnic group.] One of the popular dishes for breakfast or dinner at local restaurants is *Er kaui*—it's a patty made of rice with egg and it's stir-fried with vegetables or pork. There's also *baba*, a kind of bread. It's an easy walk—about a kilometer—to one of the crags, the Pillars, where there are sixty routes. Another area is about two kilometers away, with a number of crags near the road. If you don't feel like walking, the owner of the Faraway will give you a ride there and back for about $1.50 [USD]. You can get snacks for during the day at the local shops or the Faraway. After a day of climbing, you'll come back into town for dinner. There's not really any bars or nightlife at present. There's a Lisu cultural center in town where there's a night of singing on the weekends, but most of your entertainment comes from hanging out and chatting with other climbers."

As of this writing, it's still mostly climbers from the West who travel to Liming. Yet this is changing. "There have been three climbing festivals since I started spending time here," Mike added. "Many Chinese climbers came during the festivals. Seeing so many native climbers here was very satisfying. I've put my heart and soul into helping develop Liming. Watching an area with lots of potential grow from the ground up has been pretty special."

MICHAEL DOBIE came to China in 2010 from the Pacific Northwest. Together with the help of many climbing partners, he discovered Liming's potential and started to develop it for rock climbing. From 2011 to 2015, he spent most of his time in Liming, Keketuohai, and Western Sichuan in an effort to create traditional rock climbing opportunities for the Chinese and international climbing communities. Mike was supported by North Face China, Black Diamond, DaliBar, and Mad Rock as a professional route developer, climber, and author through this process. Currently, he splits time between the Seattle area and home in Liming. Professionally he has a degree in Athletic Training, is an AMGA single-pitch instructor, and provides outdoor educational support.

If You Go

► **Getting There:** Kunming has the nearest international airport and is served by many carriers. From Kunming, there are many carriers serving Lijang, near Liming.

► **Best Time to Visit**: October through June, with the best conditions available mid-October through November and late February through mid-May.

► **Level of Difficulty**: Liming is best appreciated by climbers of at least intermediate ability.

► **Guides**: *Liming Rock* (Michael Dobie) is a great resource. Guiding services are developing; email Mike at mdobie012@yahoo.com for details.

► **Accommodations**: The Faraway Hotel (+86 13578378448) is the main lodging spot for visiting climbers.

BLACK CANYON OF THE GUNNISON NATIONAL PARK

RECOMMENDED BY **Amos Whiting**

For adventurous, big-wall climbing in western Colorado, it doesn't get much better than the Black Canyon of the Gunnison National Park, which contains twelve miles of sheer walls of schist and gneiss stretching thousands of feet above the roaring Gunnison River.

Amos Whiting first climbed in the Black Canyon in 1996, when he was guiding out of Durango to the south. "One of my fellow guides had heard about it," Amos recalled, "and suggested we go up for a single climb, as each of us had to continue on to other commitments. There are lots of classic routes, but we were young and cocky and wanted something off the beaten path. We opted for Debutante's Ball, a grade-5 climb that's sometimes done in two days, though could be done in one long day. It's an 1,800-foot elevation gain, with some pitches to 5.11. We didn't have much information, just a hand-written topo map of the line. We camped at the top the night before, dropped down, found the base of the route, and pulled it off fall-free. I've been back many times since. Everything in the canyon is big and burly. But there's a power there, when you walk to the edge of the cliff and look into that massive chasm."

In an oft-quoted observation from 1965, a geologist named Wallace R. Hansen said:

> Several western canyons exceed the Black Canyon in overall size. . . . Some are longer, some are deeper, some are narrower, and a few have walls as steep. But no other canyon in North America combines the depth, narrowness, sheerness, and somber countenance of the Black Canyon of the Gunnison.

For the more seasoned climber, the payoff is solitude and amazing river vistas. Amos recommended a few climbs for new Black Canyon visitors. "The most popular route for

OPPOSITE:
The sheer dark
walls of the
Black Canyon
will give pause
to many
climbers . . .
not to mention
the fact that you
need to reach
the bottom before
climbing up.

13
DESTINATION

new climbers is Maiden Voyage [5.9]—a fitting name, as it's the best introduction to Black Canyon. One of its cool aspects is that you summit a tower that's set off from the canyon rim. There's a nice three-pitch add-on called King Me [5.10] that was put up by Josh Gross. The Cruise [5.10+] is another climb you can't leave out. It's twelve pitches on the North Chasm View Wall, and gets morning sun. Scenic Cruise [5.10d] is a three-pitch variation on the Cruise. It includes a Pegmatite Traverse that brings you back to the Cruise. This pink quartz-like rock gives the route its spice. It's the most famous of the 5.10 routes at Black Canyon."

Climbing a steep chasm where you must head down *before* going up can pose interesting logistical challenges. These are only increased when your day begins on the opposite rim. "My most trusted climbing partner and I were on the north rim of the canyon, and we decided that we wanted to climb Astro Dog, which is on the south rim. There's a Tyrolean Traverse that lets you get across the river. So we thought we'd do the traverse, leave our walking shoes at the base of the south chasm, climb up, rappel down, and pick them up before going back across. Astro Dog is a two-thousand-foot climb, Grade V. Dehydration can be a problem in the Black Canyon, especially on a long climb like Astro Dog. The key is to be light enough to get the climb done, but to have enough water and calories to keep you going. We were climbing well, but at the crux about two thirds of the way up, my hand began cramping from lack of water. About the same time, we came upon two ropes with gear still attached. We managed to grab all the gear. I ended up taking a fall on the next pitch but recovered. We tried carrying the rope out, but it was too heavy.

"Finally, we reached the top. There was about fifteen minutes of light left. We had twelve rappels to do, then we had to cross the river and climb up the north chasm. As I was contemplating this, my friend decided to see if he could get us a ride back around. He started chatting with a lady who was on a national park trip. She was open to giving us a ride back. We told her it was an hour. It turned out it was three hours, forty-five minutes. By the time we reached the town of Crawford, she'd had enough. She got a motel room and we walked into the local bar with our climbing shoes to see if we could convince someone to give us a ride for twenty bucks. Eventually, some guy agreed to take us. We were there by 10:30 P.M., and we paid him.

"The next morning I lost the *roshambo* and had to head down and rescue our walking shoes."

A MOS W HITING is the owner and head guide of Aspen Expeditions. He was the twentieth American to receive his IFMGA (International Federation of Mountain Guides Associations) certification, the highest level of mountain guide certification in the world. Amos has worked as an outdoor educator and guide since 1995. In the winter, he guides backcountry skiing, hut trips, and ice climbing and teaches Level I and II AIARE (American Institute for Avalanche Research and Education) courses. In the summer, he guides rock and alpine climbing. Amos has worked all over the world. He has adventured and guided in Canada, Japan, Tanzania, France, Spain, Switzerland, Italy, Mexico, Peru, Nepal, Thailand, and throughout the lower forty-eight states and Alaska. He has free climbed Moonlight Buttress (Grade V, 5.12+); onsite ascent of the Rainbow Wall Original (Route IV, 5.12a); a first ascent and ski descent of 60-degree Sick Iron in Alaska's Chugach Range; and a solo ascent of the Frendo Spur, D+, in Chamonix, France. Amos climbs Water Ice 5 and deep water solos 5.12+. In the summer he also runs a camp focused on Deep Water Soloing in Mallorca, Spain (www.mallorcaclimbingcamps.com). He is sponsored by G3 and The North Face.

If You Go

▶ **Getting There:** Montrose is less than thirty minutes from the Black Canyon of the Gunnison and is served by several carriers, including Delta (800-221-1212; www.delta.com) and United (800-864-8331; www.united.com). Montrose is about 250 miles from Denver.

▶ **Best Time to Visit**: The best conditions are found from mid-April through July and September through mid-October.

▶ **Level of Difficulty**: Only strong intermediate climbers (and above) should consider the Black Canyon.

▶ **Guides**: One guidebook is available, *The Black: A Comprehensive Climbing Guide to Black Canyon of the Gunnison National Park* (Vic Zeilman). Aspen Expeditions (970-925-7625; www.aspenexpeditions.com) leads single- and multi-day trips to the Black Canyon.

▶ **Accommodations**: There are several campgrounds in the national park (www.nps.gov /blca). Montrose has motel options, which are highlighted at www.visitmontrose.com.

RIFLE

RECOMMENDED BY **Jon Cardwell**

Jon Cardwell was introduced to Rifle Mountain Park by a young climber he kept running into at youth competitions in the early 2000s named Daniel Woods. "I was doing a lot of climbing around New Mexico, Arizona, and Colorado," Jon recalled. "Dan would be there competing, and we became friends. He suggested that I come up and meet him and his dad at Rifle. Dan had spent a lot of time there growing up, and had some early break-through there. I was twelve or thirteen at the time and just beginning to get into travel climbing. My dad and I met Dan and his dad there. I remember it being so new and excit-ing—the whole idea of traveling to a new place and being free to climb all the time. Rifle is a pretty place, an oasis in the dry, rolling hills of western Colorado. You drive through these farm fields and then wind up in this narrow slot canyon, with rock everywhere, on both sides. I wanted to climb on everything I saw . . . though once I started moving on the walls, I was intimidated. My early experience had been on granite and basalt. The lime-stone rocks here had a very different feel. But I embraced the challenge, and it helped that I had the support of friends. It wasn't long before I was doing 5.13s."

The city of Rifle sits in Garfield County, roughly two hundred miles due west of Denver, and Rifle Mountain Park is only fifteen minutes outside of town. The park was discovered by climbers in the mid-1980s. Speaking to Dougald MacDonald and *Climbing* magazine, Mark Tarrant described his early memories of Rifle: "When sport climbing hit in the mid-1980s, I thought Rifle would be just perfect, especially since all the hard routes in Europe were being done on that strange rock called limestone." Tarrant was not the first climber to make an ascent in Rifle, but he and Richard Wright bolted and climbed other firsts, including Rumor Has It (5.11a). Today, Rifle boasts more than 250 bolted routes.

OPPOSITE:
For Jon Cardwell,
Rifle comes into
its own with its
more difficult
climbs. Here,
Joel Love tackles
one of those
5.13a's, Beer Run.

14

DESTINATION

"One of the attractions of Rifle is the high concentration of easily accessible routes," Jon continued. "All the cliffs are roadside and stretch over two miles. The canyon stays relatively cool in the summer months thanks to morning and late-afternoon shade, and the creek also helps to keep things cool. Rifle has a high concentration of 5.12 to 5.14 climbs. It's those 5.14 routes that inspire me." Like many visitors to Rifle, Jon might like to start the day on Project Wall. "It's literally on the road, and since it's on the east side of the canyon, it gets morning shade," he described. "It's part of the warm-up circuit for many climbers. There's Rehabilitator, a classic 5.11, and Defenseless Betty [5.12a]. These routes are occupied every day of the week, especially on the weekends. The Meat Wall also has morning shade and some good warm-ups, including Cardinal Sin [5.12a]."

Once he's warmed up a bit, Jon will move on to some more challenging routes. "Among the 5.12s, I really like Easy Skankin'," he shared. "It was first done in the '90s and is on the Anti-Phil Wall. It's 110 feet long and requires a variety of climbing styles—technical moves, power-bouldering moves, the full package. I try to do it once or twice every year. If I take a group of kids to climb at Rifle, I'll try to get them on it. In the 5.13 category, there are lots of amazing routes. One of the best 5.13a routes is the Eighth Day, on Project Wall. It's almost two hundred feet long and goes to the top of the canyon. This was one of the first routes bolted in the canyon [by Mark Tarrant]. It follows a long blue streak up a massive orange wall. Huge [on Bauhaus Wall] is a great 5.13d route. It's a 120-foot pitch and requires both power and endurance. The 5.13ds are very challenging, but people will find one that suits them and work on it through the season.

"The 5.14s are where everything accumulates for me at Rifle. There's a 5.14a called 7 P.M. Show [at Winchester Cave]. It was first done in '95 or '96. It's some of the best rock here, but it's only forty-five or fifty feet long. Still, it's one of the better routes for the grade. Shadow Boxing [a 5.14d] is arguably the hardest route in Rifle. It's about 150 feet to the top of the wall, with several mega-pitches. It's super challenging."

Jon dedicates a good deal of his time coaching young rock climbers, and sometimes the training schedule will include a weekend at Rifle. "On a team trip one summer, I was trying Shadow Boxing on and off, as I was with the kids in the lower canyon. It was really hot, and you usually don't climb the hard routes in August. But then some wind came through, cooling things down, and I thought I should try it. The other coach encouraged me to go for it. I took two of my kids and had one belay me. Halfway through, the rest of the team drove up and were cheering me on. It wasn't the time to do Shadow Boxing, but I was climbing well, the conditions changed in a positive direction, and I had all that support. I made it."

JON CARDWELL is a professional climber, climbing coach, and route setter who resides in Boulder, Colorado. He has traveled extensively around the world in pursuit of adventure and climbing challenges. Jon has contributed new routes in South America, North America, Turkey, Europe, and China. In addition to his climbing achievements over the past fifteen years, which include international podiums, national titles, multiple 9a ascents including more than one hundred other 8b+ and harder ascents, the 3rd ascent of the Game 8C, along with dozens of problems 8B and harder, he has reserved a portion of time while at home to teach climbing and coach a youth team at his local climbing gym. Jon is one of the very few Americans to climb multiple 5.15a routes and an 8C boulder problem. He is sponsored by Adidas Terrex, Petzl, Five Ten, FrictionLabs, and Tension Climbing.

If You Go

▶ **Getting There:** Rifle is roughly three hours west of Denver. Visitors can also fly into Vail (roughly thirty-five miles away), which is served by American (800-433-7300; www.aa.com) and United (800- 864-8331; www.united.com).

▶ **Best Time to Visit**: Most climbers visit between April and mid-November, with optimal conditions in June, September, and October.

▶ **Level of Difficulty**: The most memorable climbs at Rifle are 5.9 and above. While there are routes fit for less skilled climbers, Rifle is best suited for seasoned climbers.

▶ **Guides**: *Rifle Mountain Park* (Dave Pegg) is a trusted guidebook. Several guide services are available, including the Absolute Alpine (www.theabsolutealpine.com), which is based in Rifle.

▶ **Accommodations**: There's a campground north of the canyon at Rifle Falls State Park (970-625-1607). The town of Rifle (www.riflechamber.com) has a number of motel options. Many climbers opt for Red River Inn (970-876-2346; www.redriverinnsilt.com) in nearby Silt.

LAKE DISTRICT NATIONAL PARK

RECOMMENDED BY **Richard Goodey**

The Lake District National Park sits in the northwestern corner of England in the county of Cumbria, not far from the Scottish border. The park's 885 square miles have a storybook charm that's underscored by its neat, whitewashed cottages and bucolic fields dotted with sheep, all framed by the ever-present mountains (*fells* in the local parlance). The region was sculpted out during the last Ice Age; the ice left great U-shaped valleys filled with lakes—sixteen larger lakes and hundreds of tarns. The Lake District is a national park, but not in the way that Yellowstone is a national park. It's a working environment, with villages, farms, and businesses; roughly forty thousand people live within park boundaries. Though some towns have evolved to accommodate tourism, most of the region's villages strive to preserve the England of yore and have changed very little over the past century or two.

Whatever your high school or college English class experience with "Tintern Abbey" or "The Prelude," most will agree that William Wordsworth nicely captured the romance and beauty of the Lake District in his poem "I Wandered Lonely as a Cloud":

> I wander'd lonely as a cloud
> That floats on high o'er vales and hills,
> When all at once I saw a crowd,
> A host, of golden daffodils;
> Beside the lake, beneath the trees,
> Fluttering and dancing in the breeze.

If Wordsworth's poetry helped romanticize the region, his travelogue, *Guide to the Lakes,*

OPPOSITE:
A climber takes in the view of Stickle Tarn while climbing Pavey Ark in Great Langdale.

put it on the vacationer's map. Today, the park sees over twelve million visitors annually. A modest portion of those visitors come to climb.

"I grew up in the southeast of England, and my parents took us on holidays to the Lake District," Richard Goodey shared. "My father was a climber, so we were dragged up and down different mountains and climbing routes. I've climbed over much of the world by now, but the Lake District has a special place in my heart. There's a tremendous variety of climbing to be had here, from easy-to-access roadside crags to big mountain cliffs that hold the longest routes in the country. The Lake District is also one of England's biggest scrambling venues. [Scrambling in England is part hiking, part nontechnical climbing, often along lengthy, exposed knife-edge ridgelines.] You could climb here much of your life without exhausting the possibilities."

Rock climbing has a long and storied history in the Lake District. According to the archives of the Armitt Library (located in the village of Ambleside), it was here that rock climbing developed as a sport distinct from mountaineering in the 1880s and '90s: "While Alpine mountaineering remained largely the preserve of the English upper class, the coming of the railways in the later part of the nineteenth century gave many, particularly from the northern industrial cities, access to areas such as the Lake District." The notion of a climbing club was posited around 1887 by one of the fathers of rock climbing, John Wilson Robinson. It took some time for the club to come into being, but in 1907, the Fell & Rock Climbing Club was formed at the Sun Inn in Coniston, with the mission to "encourage and foster under the safest and most helpful of conditions the exhilarating exercise and sport of Fell Rambling and Rock Climbing in the Lake District." The club continues to thrive to this day, with more than a thousand members. The club has published climbing guides to the Lake District since 1922.

There are climbing opportunities to be had throughout the Lake District, but for good rock—and the vistas of picturesque valleys and tarns that many come for—Great Langdale is a great place to start. Langdale is situated near the center of the national park and extends toward Scafell Pike, England's tallest mountain, at 3,209 feet. "One of the better-known crags in Langdale is Gimmer Crag," Richard continued. "It's highlighted in Ken Wilson's climbing books, *Classic Rock*, *Hard Rock*, and *Extreme Rock*. British climbers aspire to do all the routes here. For an easy start, there's Bracket and Slab. Going up the grade a bit is Ash-tree Slabs [5.3]. Two of the most challenging climbs at Gimmer are Kipling Groove [5.9+] and Gimmer String [5.10b]. Gimmer String has three or four pitches, on a steep line that's very exposed, very over-hanging. It's out of this world—an unreal experience but achievable by someone with average skills. White Ghyll Crag is also in the Langdale area. The climbs here—Gordian Knot, Slip Knot, Haste Not, Laugh Not—are between one hundred and two hundred feet and fairly challenging, but close to the road. A bit farther along is Pavey Ark, which has some world-class walls (up to nearly five hundred feet) with both easy and super-hard routes. Golden Slipper is a fun route for a reasonably skilled climber. It's some severely exposed slab climbing high up, both delicate and technical. If you want something even more challenging, try Poker Face; it's extreme by English standards, but a classic." Should you decide to sample a bit of scrambling, Richard recommends Striding Edge, Sharp Edge, Pinnacle Ridge, and Needle Ridge.

For climbers focusing on the Langdale region, the village of Ambleside provides a good base. "It's a bit more vibrant than the other main towns, Kendall and Keswick. There are also many camping options in Great Langdale. A nice middle path in the countryside is bunk barns. They are literally barns with bunks, a stove, and other basic amenities." An integral part of a visit to the Lake District is a pint (or two) of Real Ale at a country pub. One favorite in the valley is the Old Dungeon Ghyll. The Sticklebarn also comes recommended. "If you stay at the bunk barn in St. John's in the Vale, there's a lovely pub called the King's Head Inn. You have to walk two miles on a country road from the bunk barn to reach it." Just enough to earn your pints en route . . . and to clear your head for the next day's climbing on the way back.

RICHARD GOODEY is the co-founder of Lost Earth Adventures, which leads a variety of outdoor-oriented tours in England's Lake District and Nepal. His passion for the outdoors began at a young age when his family holidays revolved around hill walking and mountaineering in the Alps and the United Kingdom. When Richard was seventeen, his father took him on a real adventure, going on a one-month expedition to climb unclimbed peaks in the Karakoram Mountains of Pakistan. His adventures have taken him from the French Alps to the Canadian Rockies. Richard spends half the year guiding in Nepal. He's a qualified rock-climbing instructor, Mountain Leader, Level 2 Caving Leader (multi-pitch, vertical descents), and mountain bike instructor. Richard is also a white-water rescue specialist, is wilderness first aid trained, and has a Recreational Avalanche certification.

If You Go

▶ **Getting There:** The Lake District is roughly 1.5 hours north of Manchester, England, which is served by most major international carriers. There is also train service from London.

▶ **Best Time to Visit**: Mid-April to end of September is the climbing season; fewer crowds and good conditions are found in mid- to late September.

▶ **Level of Difficulty**: The climbs around the Lake District range from 5.3 to 5.14 and are mostly trad.

▶ **Guides**: There are a number of guidebooks for the Lake District, including *Lake District Rock* (Fell & Rock Climbing Club). A number of guide services are available, including Lost Earth Adventures (+44 1904500094; www.lostearthadventures.co.uk).

▶ **Accommodations**: The Lake District National Park website (www.lakedistrict.gov.uk) outlines options from campgrounds to bunk barns to country inns.

CHAMONIX

RECOMMENDED BY **François Pallandre**

Chamonix's appeals for present-day rock aficionados are many. But an equal part of the attraction is its rich past. "Chamonix has long been called 'the world capital of alpinism,' François Pallandre began. "It was around the Mont Blanc massif that the concept of alpinism was invented by the English in the nineteenth century. Even today, what impresses the visitor is the 'alpine atmosphere' that one feels when arriving in the valley. Of course, when you climb, the environment of dizzying, snowcapped peaks and glaciers is unique. Another special feature of Chamonix for the climber is the concentration and diversity of types of routes—alpine walls in red granite, multi-pitch sport crags, and even bouldering. If you wish to climb high in the mountains, there are lifts to help you access those spots."

Chamonix is situated in the southeast of France. From almost any viewpoint in the valley, Mont Blanc looms tall; at 15,782 feet, it's the highest point in the Alps, touching Italy, France, and Switzerland. Being the pinnacle of western Europe, Mont Blanc has long attracted the adventurous, be they paragliders, ice climbers, or extreme skiers.

Mont Blanc's initial ascent in 1786 that helped inaugurate the notion of alpinism was launched in part by a Genevan naturalist named Horace Bénédict de Saussure, who offered a sizable reward to anyone who could find their way to the top of Mont Blanc. Several forays ended unsuccessfully, as climbers were wary of staying overnight on the mountain, which the climb would demand. It took twenty-six years, but two local men, Jacques Balmat (who had hunted crystals on the massif and had successfully overnighted at elevation) and a Chamonix doctor named Michel Gabriel Paccard, who was more interested in scientific, rather than monetary, rewards, made the climb on August 2. It was seventy years later that the Alpine Club was formed in London; the many peaks around Chamonix would be the group's focus for years to come.

Mountaineering was certainly the focus of earlier generations of Mont Blanc climbers; today, many alpinists come for high mountain trad climbing and sport climbing on countless crags. Deciding where to set one's sights among the thousands of routes around Chamonix can be a climber's greatest challenge—should one tackle the nearly three thousand feet of granite on Petit Dru or the 1,500-foot Voie Petit, a 5.13d on Grand Capucin? François shared a few of his favorite areas. "For multi-pitch and alpine routes, I recommend the Grand Capucin area and all of the Combe Maudie region. I also like Envers des Aiguilles, Le Moine, Les Drus, Pointes Lachenal, Aiguilles Rouges, Le Brévent, and Les Perrons. For sport climbs, there are many good routes at Les Gaillands, Barberine/Gietroz, Les Chéserys, Le Ventilateur, and Bionnassay. For boulderers, Col des Montents and Glacier des Bossons are fine destinations."

What separates Chamonix from many other climbing venues is the ease and speed of many of its approaches—facilitated, of course, by the aforementioned lifts. The main lift in town—Téléphérique de l'Aiguille du Midi—climbs over nine thousand feet to the 12,605-foot Aiguille du Midi and is the primary point of entrée for Chamonix's mountaineers. Cable cars depart regularly, beginning at 6:30 A.M. Writing in *Climbing*, Julie Ellison highlights the pros and cons of such accelerated approaches: "At 60 euros for a round-trip ticket, the price is as steep as the terrain, but it turns a half-day slog into a twenty-minute ride. In America, you wake up at one A.M. and eat gloopy oatmeal by headlamp to summit Colorado's Petit Grepon, returning to the car at dusk. In Chamonix, you roll out of bed at seven A.M. to enjoy pastries in the sun, then summit the 11,854-foot Pointes Lachenal, returning to town by midafternoon." This can lead to crowds and, as Ellison points out, other problems: "By removing the approach, you gain a lot of elevation quickly, creating more potential for altitude sickness and related problems."

Incidentally, if you wish to follow in Monsieur Balmat and Dr. Paccard's footsteps to the top of Mont Blanc (at least some of their footsteps, as a cable car will spirit you part of the way), the ascent can be accomplished in as few as two days. (If you lack serious alpine experience, hiring a guide or joining an expedition is strongly recommended.)

Whether you've mounted an expedition to summit Mont Blanc or tackled some new boulder problems, hearty fare awaits you back in town. The dairy- and meat-heavy traditional cuisine here is not for the faint of heart—or, it's safe to say, for those with heart conditions. Fondue Savoyarde (with local cheeses like Emmenthal and Gruyère), raclette (a semihard cheese served heated, generally with small potatoes, cornichons, and dried meat) and charcuterie are all popular. The dish that may best typify Chamonix cuisine is Tartiflette, a casserole of potatoes, bacon, onion, double cream, and Reblochon cheese. In *Food and Wine*, chef and food personality Anthony Bourdain once wrote that Tartiflette is "evidence that you can never have too much cheese, bacon, or starch."

FRANÇOIS PALLANDRE is an alpinist, climber, skier, and mountain guide. Since 1990 he has been a member of the famous Compagnie des Guides de Chamonix. François's climbing and mountaineering adventures have taken him from Kyrgyzstan to Bolivia to Yosemite. He has seventy first ascents to his credit. In addition to guiding, François also teaches at École nationale de ski et d'alpinisme in Chamonix.

DESTINATION

If You Go

▶ **Getting There:** International visitors will generally fly into Geneva, which is roughly fifty miles from Chamonix/Mont Blanc.

▶ **Best Time to Visit**: Most of the crags/walls around Chamonix are at altitude, making the rock most reliably accessible between mid-June and mid-September.

▶ **Level of Difficulty**: There's not an abundance of beginner terrain around Chamonix; the walls and crags here are best reserved for those comfortable with 5.6 and above.

▶ **Guides**: There are a number of guidebooks for the area, including *Mont Blanc Granite* (François Damilano, Julien Desecures, and Louis Laurent) and *Chamonix: A Guide to the Best Rock Climbs and Mountain Routes Around Chamonix and Mont Blanc* (Charlie Boscoe and Jack Geldard). There are a number of guide services in Chamonix, but the oldest and most famous is Compagnie des Guides de Chamonix (+33 450530088; www.chamonix -guides.com).

▶ **Accommodations**: The Chamonix Office of Tourism (+33 450530024; www.chamonix .com) highlights lodging options throughout the valley, including campgrounds.

FONTAINEBLEAU

RECOMMENDED BY **Fabien Brones**

For some, the word "Fontainebleau" summons images of an elaborate palace (like the eponymous Chateau de Fontainebleau, which boasts 1,500 rooms and 130 acres of grounds) and hotels with aspirational ambitions. For any boulderer worth her chalk, however, Fontainebleau means only one thing—a veritable oasis of rock.

"Fontainebleau has the highest number of boulders you can find in a concentrated place anywhere," Fabien Brones began. "There are more than thirty thousand boulders that have been described. The quality of the rock is great. The abundance of boulders motivates you to climb as many as you can."

The Fontainebleau region encompasses a densely forested area that begins just forty miles south of Paris. Much of the forest here—over one hundred square miles—is protected as public forests belonging to the French state or local authorities. Here, among the oak, Scots pine, beech trees, and sandy substrate rest the sandstone edifices that first attracted climbers in the 1870s—a seemingly infinite array of slopers, crimps, roofs, high-balls, rounded mantles, slabs, compression problems . . . and just about anything else you can imagine."

Writing for *Outdoor Research*, Nik Berry noted that climbing at Fontainebleau— nicknamed "Font" by English speakers and "Bleau" by locals—began in 1874, with the arrival of the Club Alpin Français, whose members were preparing for an assault on Chamonix. Spiked shoes were used at first to scale the rocks here, then espadrilles, which provided better friction. Perhaps the most important climbing development at Fontainebleau came in the 1930s when a Parisian named Pierre Allain began bouldering there for the area's own rewards, not merely as practice for other longer ascents. It was Allain who created the high-top boot with composite rubber soles that would come to be

OPPOSITE:
Zofia Reych
tackles a project
in Fontainebleau,
arguably the
birthplace
of bouldering.

known as P.A.s and would help the next generation of climbers tackle increasingly complex boulder problems. And it was Allain and his compatriots—who came to call themselves the *Bleausards*—who realized the importance of repetition to master the moves required to scale boulders sans ropes. (They also brought along rugs or straw to soften their inevitable falls, though Allain once said that thanks to the "sandy landings" around Fontainebleau's boulders, "falls are of no consequence.")

"Bouldering at Fontainebleau has evolved a good deal in the last few decades," Fabien continued. "First, it was the adoption of crash pads, which were invented in the United States. It was a revolution. It gave climbers the chance to access new boulders that had potentially bad falls with much more safety. We also have many more foreign climbers visiting, and this has created a risk for the boulders, which are fragile. We have to pay more attention collectively, and make sure we all clean our climbing shoes and avoid climbing wet rocks. But the increase in visitors to the Bleau has also had a positive effect. People have started visiting new sectors, and this has extended our playground. Today, there are so many options, you can always find new problems, quiet places, and sectors or boulders more adapted to cold or warm days!"

One of the greatest problems that awaits an emerging Bleausard is where to start. Fortunately, there are around three hundred circuits of different problems suited for various ability levels. Each is marked with arrows, numbers, and dots . . . and there are even more unmarked problems. "Many high-level people come to try some iconic boulders, like the Big Island [8C or V15], which is one of the hardest problems, a five-star climb," Fabien added. "But others coming for 7a's have targets too. Here, you define the rules and compete with yourself at a convenient dimension. You can usually meet up with other people and climb together. You can learn from others." Is not speaking French a problem? No. "Since so many people are coming from somewhere outside of France," Fabien said, "English is the most commonly heard language."

Fontainebleau holds many magic moments for the visiting climber—a freshly baked breakfast croissant at a local *boulangerie*, the sweet scent of a primal forest as the sun climbs the sky, and the camaraderie of climbers who've assembled from points far and near to enjoy one of bouldering's meccas. But one of Fontainebleau's greatest satisfactions comes from within. "There are magic moments that happen when you are able to send a new problem you have been attempting for a while or even years," Fabien mused. "In those instances, you can feel the real 'flow sensation,' in which you are totally concentrated on your action, body sensations, and all the small details that make a differ-ence—friction, exact position of the fingers or feet, body tension, and strength. You are really out of time and space during these moments, and feel a super-rewarding sensation to have done your best and overcome something that was impossible before."

FABIEN BRONES became a Bleausard in the early 1980s, with Bleau his home terrain, as he lived close to Paris. He quit bouldering for a time when he moved to Brazil (after achieving an 8a at Bleau). But since returning to France, Fabien has married his profes-sional interests in sustainability and his love for bouldering at Fontainebleau with a new guesthouse, Bloasis. The house is a fruit of his passion for ecodesign: a modern house built with wood and other natural materials like straw, hemp, and clay and designed to be highly efficient and comfortable, and close to nature within a large garden with oak trees. Fabien's bouldering adventures have taken him to exotic sites in Brazil, and also Rocklands, South Africa, and Albarracin, Spain . . . but there is nothing like Bleau.

If You Go

► **Getting There:** The closest airport is in Orly, roughly forty minutes from Fontainebleau. Charles de Gaulle is seventy-five minutes away. Both are served by many major carriers.

► **Best Time to Visit**: Spring and fall provide the most consistent bouldering conditions.

► **Level of Difficulty**: With some thirty thousand problems, there's truly something for everyone.

► **Guides**: There are several climbing shops around Fontainebleau, including Decathalon (www.decathlon.fr) and S'cape (www.scape-shop.com). *Fontainebleau Fun Bloc* (David Atchison-Jones) provides a good primer.

► **Accommodations**: There are several campsites around Fontainbleau, including La Musardière (+33 164989191) and Malesherbes (www.camping-iledeboulancourt.com). A new option for visitors is Bloasis, located at Oncy-sur-École, a five-minute drive to Les Trois Pignons and over one hundred climbing sectors.

DESTINATION 17

FRANKENJURA

RECOMMENDED BY **Shawn Heath**

It was a job that brought Shawn Heath to northern Bavaria. But the promise of the Frankenjura certainly sweetened the deal.

"When an opportunity in Germany came up, I was very interested, as I'd enjoyed my time in the country during college," Shawn recalled. "I landed here for work, but I had quick draws and a rope in the other hand, as I'd heard a great deal about the limestone of the Frankenjura. It's a gigantic area, with over 1,500 crags—you can push your limits as high as they can go, even if you're an elite climber. Overall, there are more than ten thousand climbs here spread over more than 2,700 square miles, from totally easy to extremely difficult, with a majority around the 5.10-and-under level. In that respect, it's an everyman's sport-climbing destination. The setting is quite beautiful, hilly and wooded; when the cherry trees are blossoming in the spring, it has an almost Japanese feeling. It's quite a contrast to where I grew up in Arizona."

The Frankenjura is a bucolic setting of forested hillsides (dotted by the occasional castle) and verdant valleys resting between the cities of Bamberg, Bayreuth, and Nuremberg in southern Germany. (The northern part of this region of Bavaria is known as Franconian Switzerland (or Fränkische Schweiz), as nineteenth-century artists visiting the area found its valleys reminiscent of Switzerland.) It may be best known as the chosen home of Wolfgang Güllich, one of the greatest climbers the world has ever known. In his short, exuberant life (Güllich died after an auto accident at age thirty-one, in 1992), he put up hundreds of routes, many astonishingly difficult. In fact, four of his first ascents led to the creation of new grades, three of which—Kanal im Rücken (5.14a), Wallstreet (5.14b), and Action Directe (5.14d)—were put up in the Frankenjura. At this writing, twenty-eight years after Action Directe was first ascended, only twenty-four others have completed the

OPPOSITE:
Frankenjura
offers sport
climbers
more than
ten thousand
routes in
the forests
of Bavaria.

route. You probably won't want to try and climb it, but visitors to the Frankenjura should at least visit Waldkopt to view the route. (The Frankenjura is also the place where the concept of "redpointing"—from the German *Rotpunkt*—was introduced by local climber Kurt Albert, in the mid-1970s.)

The climbs in the Frankenjura are famous for being short and powerful, with difficult moves through one-, two-, and three-finger pockets. While this is certainly true, with many routes being less than twenty meters long, there are several taller crags offering routes up to forty meters tall, and the climbing ranges from juggy to slopery and slabby to overhanging. "Mark 'Monomaniac' Anderson [a professional climber] came out to visit a few years back from Colorado, and he commented on the quality of the rock, the lack of polish," Shawn continued. "Before coming, Mark wanted to know if he could travel with his family—if there would be a good mix of easy and advanced climbing and if transitioning between crags was difficult. I told him there was a good mix, and that the next crag is often only a short drive away, if it's not already in walking distance. When he was here, he'd choose a family-friendly crag as a warm-up and then head to something more challenging for himself. Most approaches to the crags are less than ten minutes."

A climbing day in the Frankenjura unfolds in a uniquely Bavarian manner, as Shawn explained. "You'll wake up in one of the camping areas, and order coffee and some breakfast rolls—*Brötchen*—at the campground or a nearby cafe or bakery. Brötchen are little loaves of bread; you cut them in half and put in either Nutella or jam if you want a sweet breakfast or wurst and cheese if you want savory. After fueling up, you can hike to any number of crags near the campground, or jump in the car to reach a more distant crag. You don't usually need to drive more than fifteen minutes. Trubachtal is a great area for intermediate climbers; camping at Oma Eichler's, you'll have enough in walking distance to last you through at least a week. Röthelfels, Weißenstein and Roter Fels also have good intermediate terrain. Advanced climbers will have fun at Rote Wand and the other nearby Kleinziegenfelder Tal crags, as well as at Krottenseer Turm, Bärenschlucht, and Püttlacher Wand.

"After a half day of climbing, you'll head back to camp for coffee; as Wolfgang Güllich said, coffee is a critical element of climbing. In the Frankenjura, your coffee is often served with cake. It's like English teatime with biscuits, but with coffee and cake. If you feel like you can still move after cake, you can head back to the rocks or take a walk in the woods on one of the many trails. For dinner, there are many options—Mexican, Italian, and Chinese food, all adapted for Bavarian tastes. But of course, you'll want to try the

German food. There are many different dishes, but they all boil down to meat with a brown sauce and potatoes. If you like beer, you'll want to finish the evening with a *Maßkrug* of Kellerbier, a milder style that's popular in Fränkische Schweiz. Hefeweizen is also popular. When you go into one of the beer halls, you don't have to ask for a certain brand of beer, just the type."

"The essence of the Frankenjura is working on a problem," Shawn opined. "At first, your thinking is, 'Oh, this is so hard!' You feel like those last two finger pockets are just killing your fingers. Next day you try again. Your friends are rooting you on, and you get to the anchors above the trees, and you get a view of the forest all around. When you get down, the beer afterward is a perfect treat."

SHAWN HEATH grew up in Arizona but didn't start climbing until the age of twenty in Saxon Switzerland National Park during his study abroad in Dresden, Germany. After obtaining his bachelor's degree in mechanical engineering, he accepted a position in Virginia, which allowed him to later expatriate to the German branch of the company. There, he met his wife, with whom he's raising two little climbers.

If You Go

▶ **Getting There:** The Frankenjura is roughly 1.5 hours from Munich, which is served by many carriers, and three hours from Germany's main airport, Frankfurt.

▶ **Best Time to Visit**: The most pleasant months are May, June, and October, but one can climb year-round, with the exception of the coldest months, January and February.

▶ **Level of Difficulty**: With so many routes, there's something for everyone, including more than 170 routes graded 5.14a or above.

▶ **Guides**: *Franken 1* and *Franken 2* (Gebro Verlag) mix German and English to describe many of the routes here. *Südlicher Frankenjura* (Panico Alpinverlag) is a German-only guidebook that covers the other, less famous but equally beautiful areas farther south of Nuremburg.

▶ **Accommodations**: There are a number of campgrounds in the Frankenjura. Three that are popular with climbers are Bärenschlucht, Eichler, and Zur guten Einkehr.

KALYMNOS

RECOMMENDED BY **Katie Roussos**

Many climbers who've made the trek to Kalymnos will tell you that it delivers "the whole package." Katie Roussos tends to agree.

"It begins with the quality of the rock," she shared. "It's all limestone, extremely solid, with very little loose rock. I'd say that the terrain falls into three categories—extremely overhanging rock, with blobs, tufas, and stalactites; slightly overhanging or vertical rock, with pockets and smaller tufa features; and gray slabs, sculpted by the rain, with little knobs. Kalymnos is all sport climbing, and I think it's been developed very sensibly. The bolting of routes has been done in a structured manner according to guidelines, and the bolts are close to each other and very stable. You never have to walk very far to find a crag—the average is a ten- to fifteen-minute walk. And the crags—more than eighty now, with almost four thousand routes—are all near each other, and seldom more than ten or twenty minutes' drive from the villages where most climbers stay. Once you get there, most crags have a variety of routes that are well suited to a broad range of climbing skills. Finally, you have all this unfolding on a Greek island. Most of the climbs have ocean views and, since they're primarily on the west side of the island, sunset views as well."

Kalymnos is one of the Dodecanese Islands, situated roughly 250 miles southeast of Athens in the Aegean Sea. Due to its dry, steep terrain, few plants will grow, so residents have long looked to the sea for their livelihood—diving for sponges has been a big part of the local economy for generations.

Climbing on Kalymnos is a relatively recent phenomenon, beginning for all intents and purposes with the efforts of an Italian climber named Andrea di Bari, who in 1997 put up forty-three routes with some friends in the sectors now known as Arhi, Odyssey, and Poets. When features ran in *ALP* and *Rotpunkt* magazines a few years later, the word

OPPOSITE:
Kalymnos is a
sport climber's
wonderland
that didn't see
development
until the late
1990s. Here,
Wes Miraglio
tackles Dolonas.

was out. Recognizing the potential for climbing to bring visitors to the island, Katie's husband, Aris Theodoropoulos, reached out to civic leaders to help develop a climbing infrastructure—including new routes, a multilingual website, and a climbing festival that attracts individuals from thirteen countries. One quirky characteristic of the routes on Kalymnos is that some are named for local citizens and businesses that have no direct connection to climbing. "Kalymnos isn't your typical Greek island with sand beaches and whitewashed houses," Katie explained. "We didn't have much tourism until the sport climbers began arriving. Local businesses have been very supportive of efforts to expand our climbing options. I wouldn't say that businesses have been paying the climbers who bolt the routes to use their name. Instead, the naming is more a sign of gratitude and respect for their support."

There are many trips' worth of climbs at Kalymnos. Most are single pitch, though longer ascents (up to eleven pitches) are present. Many are in the shade much of the day, making Kalymnos's heat bearable for a good part of the year. Those willing to hike a bit farther have ample opportunities to find first ascents. One new favorite crag for Katie is Arginonta Valley. "It's in a small, narrow valley that leads right out to a beach," she described. "It's in the shade almost all day. There are sixty routes in there, some vertical, some overhanging. To me, it's very similar to climbing in a gym, except with beautiful natural surroundings. It combines some of the best Kalymnos has to offer—and you can swim right afterward!"

How should one plan a Kalymnos adventure? "I'd stay on the northwest coast of the island—the villages of Armeos, Masouri, and Myrties are favored by climbers," Katie shared. "There are options for all budgets, though nothing is too expensive. There's no camping allowed, so you will need to get a place to stay. Greeks don't generally eat breakfast, but the innkeepers and café owners have adapted to visitors. You'll find eggs and tomatoes and yogurt and honey. It's nice to get to the crags by 8:30 or 9:00 at the latest. That should give you five or six hours in the shade. You should be happily exhausted by then, and it's time for a light lunch somewhere in the village. (I'd save your appetite for dinner.) Then I'd head to the beach. Our beaches are rocky, not sandy, but still very beautiful. Scuba diving and snorkeling are options. You can also take a boat across to the island of Telendos, for a coffee or beer. Of course, you can also find more crags to climb.

"Dinner is the big meal here, and if you go to one of the villages between 7:00 and 8:30, you'll find it full of other climbers—maybe some you saw at the crags! There are many good restaurants, again, all reasonably priced. If you like seafood, you'll want to try a fresh tuna steak, stewed octopus, or grilled calamari stuffed with feta cheese and spices. Stewed goat is another trademark dish. You'll see goats everywhere you go around the island. Goat's a little gamey and not for everyone, but it's a staple for the local people."

KATIE ROUSSOS is co-author of the 2019 edition of the *Kalymnos Climbing Guidebook*. Raised between the United States and Greece, she discovered climbing in her mid-thirties and it changed her life. Alongside partner Aris Theodoropoulos—a Greek mountain guide, climbing instructor, and guidebook author—Katie helps develop new sport-climbing venues in Greece, and as a result, she has climbed all over the country. She also designs and co-authors the Kalymnos and Greece climbing guidebooks with Aris, creates content for their websites ClimbKalymnos.com and ClimbGreece.com, copyedits cookbooks, and narrates virtual museum guides. Katie and Aris divide their time between Athens and their home in the shadow of the cliffs in Armeos, Kalymnos.

If You Go

▶ **Getting There:** Once you reach Athens, there are a number of ways to reach Kalymnos, involving planes, ferries, or both. Direct flights are available on Sky Express (www.skyexpress.gr).

▶ **Best Time to Visit**: The season is from late March to late November, with the months on either end providing the best conditions.

▶ **Level of Difficulty**: With so many routes, there's something for everyone at Kalymnos—with an especially generous quantity of intermediate routes.

▶ **Guides**: Aris Theodoropoulos at Climb Kalymnos (www.climbkalymnos.com) is one of Greece's foremost climbing guides. *Kalymnos Climbing Guidebook* (co-written by Theodoropoulos and Katie Roussos) is the definitive climbing resource.

▶ **Accommodations**: Discover Greece (www.discovergreece.com) lists some options in Kalymnos. Many private home rentals are available. Note that no camping is permitted.

CITY OF ROCKS

RECOMMENDED BY **Benjamin Eaton**

For "Forty-Niners" traveling the California Trail in the mid-nineteenth century, the collection of granite spires and summits they encountered north of the Great Salt Lake were a mere curiosity; their gold lay many miles west. For sport and trad climbers alike, however, the City of Rocks is a motherlode unto itself.

"One of the draws of the area is the aesthetics," Ben Eaton began. "You come around a bend in the road and it's revealed to you—a mass of gray granite stones, side by side and offset, all these amazing formations against a backdrop of junipers and smaller mountains. The stones really resemble skyscrapers—they call it City of Rocks for a reason! Another draw is the variety of the climbing experiences available. There's a good number of sport and trad climbs, and bouldering as well. It's a good place to find routes of moderate difficulty, a lot in the 5.9 to 5.11 range. Though I grew up in southeastern Idaho, about three hours away, I didn't know much about it until I was a more in-depth climber. I wasn't in a position in my climbing career to drive more than an hour to climb. The first time I went, we'd just had our first baby, and we decided to get some friends together and go to the City. It was my first rock climbing road trip. The experience of rounding that bend blew me away. I didn't know how to trad climb at first, but I tried to expand my knowledge. Now, one year I'll be gung-ho for trad climbing, another I'll focus on sport climbs. There's so much there, it's hard to get tired of it."

City of Rocks rests in south-central Idaho, just a few miles north of the border with Utah. It was designated a National Reserve in 1988, in recognition of both the significance of its geological (some of the granite spires reach heights of six hundred feet and date back 2.5 billion years) and cultural history. Hundreds of thousands of westward emigrants passed through the region en route to Granite Pass and Nevada; many left

OPPOSITE:
The granite
spires of City
of Rocks indeed
recall a cluster
of skyscrapers.

DESTINATION 20

97

their names in axle grease on rocks in the reserve, including Camp and Register Rock, and these reminders of the settlers' long trek remain today. (It was a settler named James F. Wilkins who first identified the granite edifices here as "the City of Rocks.") Long before the westward settlers passed through, the City of Rocks was the domain of the Shoshone and Bannock peoples, who hunted buffalo and collected nuts from the pinyon pines that still grow here. It's believed that the Shoshone would ascend Bath Rock and take ritual swims in the rain-/snow-filled potholes at the top.

City of Rocks has been discovered by climbers several times. Its first incarnation was as a trad climbing spot, with many routes established by a group of Utahans known as the Steinfell Club and led by Greg Lowe, who would go on to form Lowe Alpine with his brothers. At the time, the ascents here were considered equal in difficulty to some of the toughest routes at other climbing meccas like Yosemite. The City's second moment in the relative limelight came in the 1980s, when it was discovered by sport climbers. But its fame was fairly short-lived. As Dougald MacDonald noted in a piece in *Climbing*, "the best climbers moved on to newly discovered—and much steeper—sport climbs in places like Rifle, Colorado, and American Fork, Utah. What was left was an everyman's Eden."

With a mix of more than six hundred sport and trad routes within the Reserve, it can be hard to know where to start. Ben offered some advice. "Newcomers like to cut their teeth at two locations. One is the back side of Bath Rock, right off the main road in front of the main parking lot. It has a ton of bolted sport routes. Colossus [5.10c] is the go-to here, though it's a bit daunting. Rollercoaster [5.8] is another popular route. Elephant Rock is another major formation that's right off the road. It's all trad routes here. Wheat Thin [5.7] and Rye Crisp [5.8] are two climbs people will do their first time—it's hard to visit the City and not go on these routes. And chances are you'll want to do them over and over again. I'm a little weak on my slab climbing, and on a few routes on Elephant Rock, I wanted to wet myself, as there's not a lot to hold on to. I was at my mental limit, and I think that's why that sticks in my mind. One of my favorite formations at the City is Morning Glory Spire. It creates an amazing skyline; some call it Incisor, as there's a section of rock that sticks up like a canine tooth. Morning Glory [5.10c/d] is a test piece in that area, a 250-foot three-pitch ascent. When you top out, you're standing on top of a big granite tooth with a 360-degree view."

Ben Eaton's first trip to City of Rocks came from an effort to bring friends together. Eventually these little gatherings took on a life of their own. "Each year I'd set a date for

DESTINATION 20

this annual friends' climbing trip and then send a message out," he recalled. "More and more friends came, and I decided that we could invite the general public and make it a festival. Castle Rocks [another great climbing destination, just a stone's throw from City of Rocks] is the headquarters for the Idaho Mountain Festival, which tops out at 350 participants."

BENJAMIN EATON is the marketing manager for Petzl America and the founder of the Idaho Mountain Festival (www.idahomountainfestival.com). He previously served as communications specialist at Liberty Mountain, advertising and digital media sales manager at *Rock and Ice*, and race director and grassroots ambassador for Ragnar Relay Series. Ben's climbing adventures have taken him to Idaho and Utah, as well as most of the western states and Thailand.

If You Go

▶ **Getting There:** The nearest commercial airport to Almo is ninety miles distant in Twin Falls, Idaho, which is served by Delta (800-221-1212; www.delta.com). Salt Lake City is about 180 miles away and is served by most major carriers.

▶ **Best Time to Visit**: Spring through early fall offers the most consistent conditions. It can be hot in the summer, but you can usually find shaded areas to climb. If it doesn't snow, late fall can be excellent.

▶ **Level of Difficulty**: City of Rocks boasts an abundance of intermediate climbs, but there are many routes in the 5.5 to 5.7 range for less seasoned climbers . . . though note that some of the grades may seem a bit light for what they involve.

▶ **Guides**: Several guide services are permitted to operate at City of Rocks, including Sawtooth Mountain Guides (208-806-3063; sawtoothguides.com). *City of Rocks Idaho: A Climber's Guide* (Dave Bingham) is an excellent primer.

▶ **Accommodations**: There are several campgrounds in the area, including City of Rocks campground (208-824-5901; www.nps.gov/ciro). The Almo Inn (208-824-5577; www .almoinn.com) offers rooms in town.

ELEPHANT'S PERCH

RECOMMENDED BY **Kyle Goupil**

For climbers hoping to immerse themselves in the many natural wonders of Idaho's Sawtooth Mountains—and challenge themselves with some of the region's most exhilarating ascents—the massive, 1,100-foot-tall golden granite wall of Elephant's Perch beckons.

"I first learned about Elephant's Perch by reading about climbing opportunities in the Sawtooths," Kyle Goupil recalled. "It's definitely the cream of the crop there, especially if you want to have an overall outdoor adventure. There aren't any official guidebooks about Elephant's Perch. I did most of my research on MountainProject.com and by visiting a gear shop in Sun Valley that's also called Elephant's Perch. There's a binder in the shop of hand-drawn topo maps. You can take pictures of them, and the staff is happy to share information. I think the do-it-yourself research you need to do to climb Elephant's Perch keeps the crowds away and gives you an added sense of adventure."

The Sawtooth National Recreation Area stretches over 750,000 acres of mostly undeveloped country in central Idaho, beginning just northwest of the resort area of Sun Valley. The region includes forty peaks eclipsing ten thousand feet and more than three hundred alpine lakes. Redfish Lake, where Elephant's Perch adventures begin (near the town of Stanley), is one of the Sawtooth's jewels. The five-mile-long, crystalline lake takes its name from the vast numbers of sockeye salmon that once migrated here from the Pacific, a voyage of some nine hundred miles (the longest migration of any salmon species). The story goes that at one point in time, the sockeye—which turn bright red as they approach their spawning period and death—were so thick that the water turned red. (Dams on the Columbia and Snake River systems nearly drove Redfish Lake sockeye to extinction; some might recall "Lonesome Larry," the single salmon that returned to the lake in 1991. Returns have improved somewhat, though remain a shadow of historic runs.)

OPPOSITE: Those who've made the trek to Elephant's Perch generally agree that it's one of the jewels of the Sawtooth Mountains.

The first recorded ascents in the Sawtooths—named for their steep, jagged peaks—were logged by Bob and Miriam Underhill, in the mid-1930s. The Underhills, who brought rope techniques they'd witnessed in the Alps to American climbing, notched some twenty first ascents here over the course of several visits. Paul Petzoldt, who founded the National Outdoor Leadership School, passed through the Sawtooths, bagging Warbonnet Peak along the way. It was the legendary Fred Beckey who put up the first ascent on Elephant's Perch. Beckey first came to the Sawtooths in 1949. It was some years later, in 1963, that he climbed the route that came to bear his name, along with Steve Marts and Herb Swedlund: Original Beckey (5.11). A newer version of the route, established in 1983, is called Direct Beckey (5.11b).

It was an eight-mile bushwhack to reach Elephant's Perch when Beckey first conquered it. It's a bit easier now. Kyle described how he and his climbing partners will typically mount an expedition: "We'll leave Salt Lake City early and stop in Sun Valley or Ketchum and grab some food. From there, we'll head on to Redfish Lake. You can hike around the lake to the trailhead that leads up to base camp, or you can take a boat shuttle across the lake for twelve dollars. The boat is a lot faster and adds another element of adventure, and the scenery from the water [including vistas of Grand Mogul (elevation 9,733 feet) and Mount Heyburn (elevation 10,239 feet)] is tremendous. From the other end of the lake, it's a roughly three-mile hike to the campsite. Even if you catch the last shuttle, which leaves at seven P.M., you should have enough light to get to the site. [Though it's less than three miles, the hike in is rigorous, gaining almost two thousand feet in elevation.] On one side there's Elephant's Perch, this huge granite dome. On the other, you have the Saddleback Lakes. Between the views—including the reflection of the Perch on the lake—and the proximity to the climbing routes, this camp checks a lot of boxes."

When you wake up the next morning, thirty different routes await you after a brief hike up from your camp near the lake. The most popular (and least difficult) is the Mountaineer's Route (5.9), which was first established in 1967 by Gordon Webster, T. M. Herbert, and Dennis Hennek. "Though it's the easiest on the wall, it's still a serious undertaking," Kyle shared. "It heads up the left side of the wall over eight pitches, and provides fun, moderate climbing. Mountaineer's was my first ascent at Elephant's Perch. My favorite is Direct Beckey. It takes a beautiful line on one continuous crack, from the base to the top of the dome. It's about twelve pitches total, and you're climbing about 1,100 feet. You're in it start to finish. Direct Beckey doesn't let off until you're right at the top. The average climber will take ten hours to do the route, and then another hour or so to get back down to the bottom. The other must-dos are Myopia [5.11a] and the Fine Line [5.11c]."

The day that Kyle conquered Direct Beckey has stayed with him. "It was the first hard alpine rock climb my partner and I had done," he reminisced. "I loved the final pitch. When I topped out and belayed my partner up, I was thinking, 'All right—what else is possible?' It was hard, but not as hard as we expected. Completing the climb made me excited for what else was out there. Sitting at camp that night, the trout came out to feed on bugs on the surface of the lake. It looked like it was raining as the sun set."

KYLE GOUPIL is an avid climber residing in Salt Lake City with his wife and dog.

If You Go

▶ **Getting There:** Visitors can fly into Boise, which is served by many carriers; from here it's a roughly three-hour (130-mile) drive to Redfish Lake.

▶ **Best Time to Visit**: Mid-June through mid-September offers the best conditions, though thunderstorms can crop up suddenly and snow can fall almost any time.

▶ **Level of Difficulty**: The ascents at Elephant's Perch are fairly stout and best reserved for climbers of at least intermediate experience.

▶ **Guides**: Several outfits lead climbs on Elephant's Perch, including Sawtooth Mountain Guides (208-806-3063; www.sawtoothguides.com).

▶ **Accommodations**: You'll need to overnight in the primitive (but beautiful) campground below Elephant's Perch. Before and after your ascent, there are many campgrounds around Redfish Lake (877-444-6777; www.recreation.gov). The Stanley Chamber of Commerce (www.stanleycc.org) lists lodging options in town.

ARCO

RECOMMENDED BY **Matteo Pavana**

What makes Arco one of Europe's most celebrated sport climbing destinations? Is it the abundance of limestone *falesie* (crags), begging to be ascended? Is it the proximity of Lake Garda, one of Italy's most popular tourist attractions? The mild climate? Or is it the annual Rock Master competition, which attracts many of the world's most talented competitive climbers? For Matteo Pavana, the answer is simple: "Arco is Arco. There's nothing like this small village rising between the Brenta Dolomites in the north and Lake Garda in the south. You can relax just by walking its tiny streets while having a handcrafted gelato; you can hike; you can go boating on the lake. And, of course, you can climb hard."

Arco is a small town in the northern Italian province of Trentino, situated at the northern tip of Lake Garda. The area—which from a climbing perspective extends from the town northeast up the Sarca River Valley to the town of Trento—boasts scores of crags, with thousands of single-pitch sport climbing routes, hundreds of multi-pitch alpine climbing routes, and hundreds of bouldering problems. "The sport climbing options in Arco are endless, starting with old-school climbing on vertical and slabby routes and ending on more futuristic walls, more athletic and overhanging routes," Matteo added.

Climbers began exploring Arco and the Sarca Valley in the 1930s, drawn from the Dolomites in the north by the hospitable climate and tall limestone walls. Early climbers here included Cesare Maestri and Reinhold Messner. Sport climbing arrived in Arco in 1982 when Austrian climber Heinz Mariacher bolted a variation on a route called Renata Rossi (5.11a). As shorter sport routes became more accepted by the climbing community, more bolted routes emerged around Arco. These routes attracted the finest climbers of the day, including Wolfgang Güllich, Jerry Moffatt, and Ron Fawcett. Soon after, Arco became known as ground zero for European sport climbing.

OPPOSITE:
Arco is home of
the Rock Master
event and a sport
climbing mecca
near Lake Garda.

"Rock climbing has grown pretty fast [in Italy] in the past few years," Matteo explained. "Many, many people are going to the climbing gym, but most of the time those people don't go outdoor climbing. In Italy, climbing is still considered a somewhat dangerous sport for families. What I can say for sure is that there are many more foreign families that climb around Arco than Italian families."

Some of the crags at Arco are extremely convenient to town, like Monte Colodri and Calvario. Thanks to the easy access, these venues tend to see more traffic than others. Matteo prefers less busy crags. "I really like the crags in the region between Trento and Arco, at the beginning of the Sarca Valley and Valle dei Laghi," he continued. "These include Monte Terlago, La Finestra, Ranzo, and Bassilandia. My two favorite crags are Padaro and Nago." 27crags.com has called Padaro "the future of Arco. It is the crag that in the last years has been developed the most and now counts over 150 routes. But further work is still planned, so Padaro will continue to grow." Padaro offers both long and technical slabs and nice overhangs, and fine views across the Alto Garda valley.

For many—especially those in the competitive climbing world—Arco is synonymous with the annual Rock Master Festival. The event was created in 1986 to bring together the planet's top-ranked climbers to compete in onsighting and roped climbing. The initial event was held on the Colodri wall, which is near the downtown area. Since 1988, all events have been held on artificial walls erected in front of the Colodri. Bouldering has been added over the years. One of the most exciting events for the thousands of spectators who flock to Arco (eight thousand in 2017) is the Rock Master Duel, where two climbers compete against each other on two identical, parallel routes. The competitor who climbs to the top first eliminates the other, until only one climber remains—the winner.

When you need a break from rocks, many fine outdoor opportunities await. "Lake Garda is famous for its windsurfing and sailing," Matteo enthused, "and there's also good trekking, via *ferrata* ['iron road,' which provides rungs, rails, and cables that permit hikers lacking technical rock climbing experience to scale rock faces] and BASE jumping." A favorite excursion for visitors is a trip to Isola del Garda, an island in the lake's southwestern section that is rich in both beauty and history. St. Francis of Assisi visited the island around 1220. Recognizing its isolation from the hubbub of daily life, he established a simple hermitage there for his monks. The island stayed in church hands for the next five hundred years and eventually came into private ownership.

DESTINATION **22**

Italy is a land of gastronomic delights, and Arco is no different. Olives, one of the most important crops in the area, are pressed to make extra virgin olive oil. Lake Garda is also known for its lemons, which find their way into a number of local recipes, including lemon cream, a popular soft drink, and Limoncino liqueur. At the dinner table, you may encounter *salada*, a salted beef that's often served raw, and tortellini, delicate handmade pasta rings filled with meat or cheese and served with melted butter, sage, and Parmesan, or in soup. Any Lake Garda meal can be enhanced with one of the fine wines produced in the area, which include Nosiola, Cabernet, Vino Santo, and Classico Groppello della Valtenesi. Finish the evening with a glass of grappa, a favorite aperitif.

MATTEO PAVANA is a photographer, filmmaker, author, and rock climber based in Trento, Italy. His photography and films have earned many awards; the film *Slaintè* was a finalist at the Orobie and Verona Film Festivals, and he received the La Sportiva Anniversary Prize at Arco Rock Star, a celebration of rock climbing photography. Matteo is also the author of three editions of *Arco Sport Climbing*, a guidebook for the region.

If You Go

▶ **Getting There:** Arco is roughly sixty miles from Verona, which has service from many European cities.

▶ **Best Time to Visit**: February through April and September through November are the best climbing seasons, though Arco is temperate enough for year-round climbing.

▶ **Level of Difficulty**: There's a broad range of climbing here, and approaches are generally short.

▶ **Guides**: A number of guidebooks are available for Arco, including *Arco Sport Climbing* (Matteo Pavana). Several guide services lead climbers in the area, including Arco Mountain Guide (www.arcomountainguide.com).

▶ **Accommodations**: There are several campgrounds in Arco, including Zoo Camping (+39 0464 516232; www.campingzoo.it) and Campeggio Arco (+39 0464517491; arco@ arcoturistica.com). Visit www.trentino.com for an overview of other lodging options.

DESTINATION 22

RED RIVER GORGE

RECOMMENDED BY **Andrew Reed**

The sandstone cliffs of the Red River Gorge in east-central Kentucky are one of America's climbing treasures. "I think the climbing is so unique here thanks to the angle of the cliffs," Andrew Reed began. "Many of the routes are steep and require very dynamic, powerful, gymnastic movements. You don't see this style of climbing in many other places—although Kalymnos, Greece, and Rifle [Colorado] come to mind. The Red has many attractive features—pockets, plates, and iron oxide bands that create a variety of holds from deep buckets to solid incut crimps. The colors in the rock swirl from bright orange to dark gray. This geology draws people from around the world."

From a climbing perspective, the Red River Gorge is spread across a large area. Some of the climbs are contained within the Daniel Boone National Forest, a swath of more than seven hundred thousand acres of federal land. "The popular crags located within the national forest are mostly in the northern and eastern parts of the Red River Gorge," Andrew continued. "Some of the best climbing is on privately owned parcels. You have Muir Valley, which is four hundred acres. And there's the Pendergrass-Murray, Miller Fork, and Bald Rock Recreational Preserves, which are owned by the Red River Gorge Climbers' Coalition and total more than one thousand acres."

Though climbers were visiting the Gorge as early as the 1950s, traffic really increased in the 1990s with the arrival of sport climbing. Kentuckians have long relied on extractive industries for their livelihood, and it's no different around the gorge. Initially, the growing procession of climbers met resistance from the region's oil and gas workers. But all parties have learned to coexist. "We wouldn't have access to many of the areas we climb if the oil and gas companies had not cut roads in," Andrew said. "I'd say that the relationship between the companies and climbers has been steadily improving."

*OPPOSITE:
Some of the
Red River Gorge
is owned by
the Red River
Gorge Climbers'
Coalition.
Here, Zoe
Bundros climbs
Mississippi Moon.*

23

DESTINATION

The Red has no shortage of celebrated sport climbs, though there are also first-rate trad routes. Andrew shared a few that visitors often attempt. "One of the older routes that people flock to is Twinkie [5.12a sport climb at Phantasia cliff]. There's almost always a line there during the peak season. The Motherlode is a world-famous piece of rock and boasts one of the most densely packed assortment of steep, quality climbs anywhere." Most of the Motherlode's routes are 5.12 and above, and so are best tackled by more skilled climbers. One of Andrew's favorite climbs, Inhibitor [5.11a], is at Eastern Sky Bridge Ridge. "It's a trad climb that I saved to get on until I was ready. It has a reputation for being hard and scary. You need crack climbing skills for a wide range of sizes. Another trad climb that takes up a lot of mental space for me is All That Glitters [5.12c] at the Gallery. In terms of my favorite places to sport climb, I really like the crags in the Sore Heel Hollow part of the PMRP, namely, the Solar Collector."

With lower temperatures and humidity, fall is one of the best times to climb in the Red River Gorge. If you visit in October, you may have the chance to partake in Rocktoberfest, a weekend-long celebration of climbing that's organized by the Red River Gorge Climbers' Coalition. "We invite outdoor brands from all over to set up booths, do demos, and promote their products," Andrew described. "We also have pro climbers host clinics to help visitors hone a variety of skills—sport, trad, the mental aspects of redpointing, etc. There's also a sport climbing competition. Competitors score points based on the number of different bolts they clip; the more routes you complete, the higher your score. For me, Rocktoberfest underscores the wonderful community that's sprung up around Red River Gorge and the Climbers' Coalition."

When Rocktoberfest isn't in session, Miguel's Pizza is the unofficial epicenter of the climbing scene. "Miguel's has been around since the beginning," Andrew added. "It's evolved into a climbing complex. If you come down without a partner, you can find one at Miguel's. You can camp, eat, get a shower—and there's a gear shop there now too. And they have good rice bowls in addition to pizza."

For many, the Red River Gorge represents one of America's premier climbing venues. For Andrew, it speaks to all that is wonderful about Kentucky. "I lived in Colorado for many years," he recalled. "When I moved back to Kentucky, I had some remorse. I missed the fly fishing, the big routes in the Rockies, and the proximity to other great climbing places in the West. Not long after coming back, I pitched a tent on the banks of Indian Creek off Forest Road 9, in the northern part of the gorge. I had brought a fly rod along, as the creek is seasonally stocked with trout. That Saturday, I caught some fish, did some hiking and some climbing. On Sunday, some friends—including my dog Ash—and I canoed the Red River. That weekend, I was able to appreciate a bit of everything the gorge has to offer—not just world-class climbing, but all the other wonderful outdoor activities. This was important, as it allowed me to become enthusiastic again about living in Kentucky. I attribute my comfort with being back home to the Red River Gorge."

ANDREW REED serves on the board of directors for the Red River Gorge Climbers' Coalition. A Louisville resident, he learned to climb in the Red in 2008. He has an MS in biology from the University of Colorado and is passionate about land and natural resource conservation. Andrew's favorite places to climb include Black Canyon of the Gunnison National Park, Rocky Mountain National Park, Yosemite National Park, Indian Creek, South Platte, and, of course, the Red.

If You Go

▶ **Getting There:** The nearest large airport is in Lexington, Kentucky, which is served by many carriers. From Lexington, it's roughly an hour's drive to Slade.

▶ **Best Time to Visit**: Spring and fall are prime time, though some will climb in the summer despite tough rock conditions.

▶ **Level of Difficulty**: There are many challenging routes—sport and trad—at Red River Gorge, but there are also a good number of ascents better suited for more modest climbers.

▶ **Guides**: The Red River Gorge Climbers' Coalition lists local guides at www.rrgcc.org /rrg-info/guides.

▶ **Accommodations**: Many climbers opt to camp on the grounds at Miguel's Pizza. Red River Gorge Tourism (www.redrivergorgetourism.com) highlights other options in the region.

ACADIA NATIONAL PARK

RECOMMENDED BY **Jon Tierney**

If you're hoping to get an early start on your climbing day, look no further than Acadia National Park, which is one of the first places in America to see the summer sunrise. As it turns out, there are few better places to climb over the ocean in North America than Acadia.

"Acadia is a place where the mountains meet the sea," Jon Tierney began. "There are very few opportunities to climb overlooking the ocean in the United States. You really have to visit remote reaches of Canada or go abroad. It's unique in that respect, especially in the Northeast. At Acadia, you can climb on sea cliffs that are directly above the Atlantic, or on walls with a view of the sea a half-mile away. Though the highest point in Acadia is only 1,500 feet, it has an alpine feeling. On some summits, you're above the tree line. It's the best of multiple worlds."

Acadia National Park's granite headlands, rocky beaches, and spruce-fir forests rest roughly three quarters of the way up Maine's sprawling coastline, and an hour's drive southeast from the city of Bangor. Spanning forty-nine thousand acres, it was the first national park established east of the Mississippi.

Acadia's out-of-the-way location and its popularity with millions of visitors content to simply *look* at the rocks have conspired to keep it below some climbers' radars. But a few early climbers saw the potential. Jeff Butterfield, who would go on to author a guidebook, was especially prolific in putting up routes. Today there are more than three hundred climbs in Acadia, mostly trad. Given the park's notoriety for seaside climbing, it's no surprise that Otter Cliffs is high on many visitors' lists. "There are some classic single-pitch climbs at Otter Cliffs, ranging from easy [5.3/5.4] to more challenging [5.11/5.12]," Jon continued. "Before going, you should know that you'll probably need to belay from

OPPOSITE: Most of the climbs at Acadia are either above the Atlantic or with the ocean in view.

24

DESTINATION

the top. It's not easy to belay from the bottom if the tide is high. Great Head holds some other fine sea cliff climbs, though it's a longer approach, you need low tides to get in, and the routes are more challenging."

Moving a bit inland—but still in view of the ocean—is the Precipice, which is better known among climbers as the South Wall. "This is where you'll find much of Acadia's elite climbing," Jon said. "It's striking pink granite, with great corners and cracks. Most of the climbs here are 200 to 250 feet, broken up into two or three pitches. You can sample many different routes here in the course of a day; if you can climb to 5.6, you can get to the top. Story of O is a great 5.6; at 5.7+, Old Town is a favorite; Return to Forever is a classic 5.9 that starts mid-cliff; and at 5.10, Fear of Flying is an exquisite route.

"A really nice thing about Acadia from a climbing perspective is that there's truly terrain for everyone. There are some places where if you can't climb well and hard, you're just going to stare at the cliff. Here, I can take someone out who's never touched rock before, and they can be climbing right next door to people who climb at 5.11. There are also so many great options for rest days—sea kayaking, whale watching, biking, and hiking. Like the climbing, there are hiking trails for people of all abilities." You can also set a very early alarm and drive to the top of Mount Cadillac to watch that early sunrise.

For many visitors to "downeast" Maine, the trip is not complete without an opportunity to tie on a bib and tuck into a fresh lobster. In 2018 (the most recent year for which statistics are available as of this writing), more than 119 million pounds of lobster were harvested from Maine waters, with many of these succulent crustaceans coming from the cold, nutrient-rich waters off Mount Desert island. Plated *Homarus americanus* can take infinite forms, but in these parts, locals prefer it simple—that is, steamed in shell and served with sides of melted butter and lemon. Most eateries in nearby Bar Harbor feature lobster, but you needn't stray far from the cliffs, as lobster is on the menu at Jordan Pond House, right in the park. The original Jordan Pond House dates back more than one hundred years; the present restaurant is set up as a teahouse, right on the shores of Jordan Pond. There's a big lawn in front of the house rolling down to the pond, and people can eat outside at picnic tables. Jordan Pond House is also known for its popovers, a tradition that goes back as long as the restaurant has been in existence. The view from here is one of the classic Acadia vistas, looking over Jordan Pond with the Bubbles in the distance and framed by the Pemetic and Penobscot Mountains.

JON TIERNEY is certified internationally by the UIAGM/IFMGA and examined and certified at the highest international standard by the AMGA as a rock guide, alpine guide, and ski mountaineering guide. He began climbing as a teenager in the mid-'70s and came to Maine in 1982 and fell in love with the pink granite of Acadia. In 1984, he co-founded Maine Bound, the University of Maine outdoor program, which he directed until 2001. In 1993, Jon established Acadia Mountain Guides, now a year-round guide service offering rock climbing, ice climbing, and mountaineering instruction. He's bagged more than seventy high-altitude peaks as well as difficult first-ascent rock and ice climbs and hundreds of multi-pitch rock and alpine routes around the world. Jon has served multiple terms on the AMGA board of directors and was the chair of the AMGA accreditation program for several years. Jon is also flight paramedic with LifeFlight of Maine. He has been a paramedic for twenty-five years, working for the National Park Service as a back-country climbing ranger in Rocky Mountain National Park, as well as in numerous urban and rural medical care systems.

24

DESTINATION

If You Go

▶ **Getting There:** Acadia is about fifty miles from Bangor, which is served by several carriers, including Delta (800-221-1212; www.delta.com). It's approximately 150 miles north of Portland, which is served by many carriers.

▶ **Best Time to Visit**: Late April to late October is the climbing season, with September often the best month.

▶ **Level of Difficulty**: There are options here for climbers of all abilities.

▶ **Guides**: *Rock Climbs of Acadia* (Grant Simmons) is the most recently published guide. Several entities offer guided climbs in the park, including Acadia Mountain Guides (888-232-9559; www.acadiamountainguides.com).

▶ **Accommodations**: There are two campgrounds in Acadia, Blackwoods and Seawall. Reservations can be made through the National Recreation Service (877-444-6777; www.recreation.gov). The Bar Harbor Chamber of Commerce (www.visitbarharbor.com) highlights other nearby lodging options.

BAXTER STATE PARK

RECOMMENDED BY **Steve Wright-Eaton**

"Every crag has its premier line," Steve Wright-Eaton began. "It's not necessarily the toughest line, but the one that's considered a classic. In Baxter State Park, on Mount Katahdin, that line is the Armadillo. At 5.7+, it's relatively accessible. It offers a diversity of climbing styles—chimney, face, and crack. It offers some of the best exposure in the east and tops out just below the summit of Katahdin. And when you reach the top, you're at the end of the Appalachian Trail."

Baxter State Park occupies a 209,501-acre swath of north-central Maine. Once the domain of the Wabanaki Native American tribe, moose, and the Great Northern Paper Company, the region's mountains, lakes, and overall potential as a nature lover's paradise first came to the attention of Percival Baxter, scion of a wealthy Portland family, in 1903 during a fishing trip. Baxter was taken with the area's beauty and utter wildness. When he became governor, he tried to convince the state to protect the land but was unsuccessful. His opportunity came with the crash of 1929. In 1930, the cash-poor Great Northern Paper Company agreed to sell Baxter the six thousand acres of land that included Mount Katahdin, for $25,000. Baxter in turn deeded this land to the state of Maine, with the proviso that the land "shall forever be used for public park and recreational purposes, shall be forever left in the natural wild state, shall forever be kept as a sanctuary for wild beasts and birds, that no road or ways for motor vehicles shall hereafter ever be constructed thereon or therein."

Baxter's assertion that Katahdin would one day be viewed as the state of Maine's crowning glory received a most powerful endorsement a few years back when L.L. Bean adopted, as a part of its logo, an illustration of the mountain—and, by extension, the Armadillo line, which is located toward the middle of the peak.

OPPOSITE:
Steve Wright-Eaton approaches the top of the Armadillo, Mount Katahdin's premier line.

DESTINATION

25

Katahdin may be the East Coast's best answer to climbing in the Rockies, though it's still a bit under the radar. There are two large basins here, the South and the North. While the North is larger, the South has more established routes, and hence sees more climbers. A number of routes are documented here—Waterfall Buttress, Pamola IV (both two thousand feet), and the Flatiron among them—but local climbers have established a number of others and tend to keep them close to their chest. It's all traditional climbing on Mount Katahdin, with no fixed bolts. And you won't find a formal guidebook to show you the way.

Part of the challenge of tackling the Armadillo is merely getting to the wall. Most climbers will try to reserve a lean-to at the Chimney Pond Campground the night before their ascent, a three-mile hike in from the parking lot. "When you get to Chimney Pond, you can see the wall," Steve recalled. "It seems ominous and imposing—it certainly gets you thinking about the next day. We got an early start for our ascent, as we were there in October and wanted to take advantage of the daylight. You need to check in with the park rangers before beginning to make sure you have the right gear. [Climbing is tightly regulated at Baxter State Park.] It's a bit of a hike before you begin climbing. You follow a dry streambed for a while. On the last half of the approach before reaching the wall, you have some steep bushwhacking up five-, ten-, twenty-five-foot rock faces. The whole time, we're watching the Armadillo get bigger. What seemed like a little buttress was suddenly two thousand feet tall! My partner and I had done some big walls before and felt we had the climbing skills, but it was still unnerving."

The Armadillo is generally broken down into six pitches. "The first pitch is in the chimney section," Steve described. "We broke that first section into two pitches to eliminate rope drag. As chimneys go, it's pretty gentle. Next, we traversed out onto the face. This was one of the most nerve-wracking moments I've had thus far in my climbing career, going from the cozy chimney to a very exposed spot six hundred feet above the floor. I'd felt comfortable doing 5.12s in the gym, but this 5.7 in the wild was another story. I had the 'Elvis leg' going. The face tops out at Armadillo Buttress. From here, it's up a sixty-foot crack. There's less exposure, so you can cool your heels a bit. Instead of protecting the belay anchor with several cams, we wrapped the protruding rock with a piece of webbing and a single stopper. At the top of the crack, you pop out at a little zen garden ledge that's very protected. Here, you can take a deep breath and take in the valley below. From here, there's a ledge of fifteen feet above the crack. After that pitch, things level out. There's one semitechnical step section along the Knife's Edge; the rocks are a bit loose here. We were losing light, so didn't make it all the way to Baxter Peak. We took the Dudley Trail down, a gentle descent. Hiking down Dudley, we had great views of Armadillo. It was cool to see it so clearly after just having ascended that face."

STEVE WRIGHT-EATON currently works in merchandising at L.L. Bean in Freeport, Maine. He has been an avid climber since his college days at Keene State, and his adventures have taken him from Seneca Rocks in West Virginia to the West Buttress of Denali in Alaska. When not climbing, Steve enjoys paragliding, skiing, paddling, and spending time with his wife, Shannon, and two dogs, Abbie and Orla.

If You Go

▶ **Getting There:** Baxter State Park is approximately 160 miles north of Portland, which is served by many carriers, including Delta (800-221-1212; www.delta.com) and United (800-864-8331; www.united.com).

▶ **Best Time to Visit:** June through mid-October is the prime rock climbing season here. You'll need to check in with rangers early on the morning of your climb; latecomers may be turned away.

▶ **Level of Difficulty:** Armadillo is a 5.7+, though its exposure belies its technical challenges. There are a range of other traditional climbs in the South and the North.

▶ **Guides:** Several outfitters offer guided climbs on Mount Katahdin, including Synnott Mountain Guides (603-733-8416; www.newhampshireclimbing.com).

▶ **Accommodations:** There are ten campgrounds in Baxter State Park (www.baxterstate park.org), some (like Chimney Pond) with lean-tos. The Katahdin Chamber of Commerce (www.katahdinmaine.com) lists motel options in surrounding towns like Millinocket.

EL POTRERO CHICO

RECOMMENDED BY **Frank Madden**

Come winter in many parts of the United States, sport climbers either renew their climbing gym memberships or trade in their shoes for skis. Another option—and a very good one—would be to head south to the town of Hidalgo in the state of Nuevo León, Mexico, to El Potrero Chico, perhaps the largest big-wall sport climbing destination in the world.

"I was getting ready to travel to the World Cup in Brazil, and was planning on doing some climbing in Central America on the way," Frank Madden recalled. "A friend said I should check out Potrero Chico. As you're approaching Hidalgo from Monterrey, there's a striking contrast between the valley and the towering walls of Potrero Chico. For people who come in on a cloudy day or at night and wake up the next morning to see the jaw-droppingly massive cliff, it's almost overwhelming. Potrero Chico is known for its big climbs—some are fifteen pitches, some over twenty. If you wanted to, you could get in one hundred pitches climbing just five or six routes over a few days. Walking five minutes from your car, you can climb one thousand feet."

El Potrero Chico is roughly 120 miles from the U.S. border at McAllen, Texas, in the eastern Sierra Madre. The region was originally known as the headquarters of the multinational cement company that would become Cemex. The steep limestone walls here—some as tall as two thousand feet—were identified for their climbing potential in the late 1980s by Alex Catlin and Jeff Jackson. By the early 1990s, other Potrero pioneers—among them "Magic" Ed Wright, who bolted more than eighty routes—were putting up tough but accessible sport climbs around the "Little Corral." There are now more than six hundred. "El Potrero is known for its moderate climbs, many in the 5.10 range," Frank continued. "The most popular route for intermediate climbers is probably *Estrellita*, or 'little star.' It's a 5.10b—though variations can take it to 5.10d—and is twelve pitches; the average climber

OPPOSITE:
*Jenna Balinski
climbs Texas
Tumble on
the Dihedrals
crag at
El Potrero.*

DESTINATION

26

can get up and down in five or so hours. There's a lone palm tree up on the summit, and climbers love to get their picture taken up there. It's a pretty easy climb for people with multi-pitch experience, though you're up 1,200 feet. El Sendero Luminoso—"The Shining Path"—is a prestigious 5.12d route for more advanced climbers. It's a commitment, 1,750 feet, and has fifteen pitches; some people will bivy overnight about halfway up." If you find yourself at El Potrero with less of a hunger for multi-pitch routes, there are many single-pitch climbs available—both slab/vertical and overhanging rock.

It's safe to say that the overall vibe at El Potrero Chico is different than what you might encounter at most sport climbing centers. "It's one of the most welcoming, low-key climbing communities I've ever found," Frank said. "It's not on the pro climber circuit, and there aren't any groundbreaking routes here—nothing over 5.13d yet. For those reasons, you don't get the really technically oriented hard-core climbers here, so there's not as much ego. A newer climber can sit down with some folks who have a lot more experience and feel welcome. The connection to the local community also makes El Potrero special. People from Hidalgo will come up to the canyon to watch the 'crazy climbers.' They'll be blasting mariachi music and have a cooler of beer. When you come off the wall, they might share a Tecate or a shot of tequila. The connection between the climbers and the Hidalgo community is largely thanks to a local man named Homero Gutierrez Villarreal, who befriended early climbers.

"His home grew into the original climber campground at El Potrero, complete with a restaurant," Frank added. "Other families followed suit, with little campgrounds and restaurants. Though Homero died in 2014, the tight-knit community remains. The local people envelop the climbers in a big hug. The longer you stay, the closer you get to the families. You really feel at home."

The hearty meals you'll find around El Potrero Chico will further strengthen your ties to the place. "Many of the meals are served taco style—meaning your *pollo asado, carne asado*, or *cabra* [goat] is served on a plate with corn tortillas, and you fill up the tortillas and eat," Frank described. "There are a few places where you can get a taco or burrito and a margarita on the way down to town from the canyon. There are several places with great tamales, including Tamale Esperanza. And there's a lady who makes massive hamburgers the size of a dinner plate that can easily feed two people. The sign out front says 'Hamburguesas y Tortas,' but everyone calls it 'Face Burger.' They cost about one hundred pesos [at this writing, about five dollars].

"The end of a climbing day at El Potrero is so satisfying. You sit down in camp or at a little cantina and have that first margarita or cold beer, waiting for your food to cook. You're surrounded by other climbers from all over the States and beyond, and everyone's in a joyful mood. And you're looking up at the mountain that you were climbing just a few hours before."

FRANK MADDEN started his climbing career in the Red River Gorge of Kentucky. He eventually found his way to the walls of El Potrero Chico. Though the nature of the climbing there couldn't be more different than his years climbing in Red River Gorge, he fell in love. Frank's love affair with EPC's tall limestone walls led him to write his first guidebook, *EPC Climbing: A Climber's Guide to El Potrero Chico*.

If You Go

▶ **Getting There:** The nearest airport (about an hour east of Potrero Chico) is in Monterrey, which is served by many carriers. From Monterrey, it's roughly forty-five minutes to Hidalgo. (Bus transportation and rental cars are available.)

▶ **Best Time to Visit**: Conditions are best between November and May, with December through February prime time.

▶ **Level of Difficulty**: There are climbs from 5.7 to 5.14, single- and multi-pitch—so most sport climbers will find some good routes here.

▶ **Guides**: Several guidebooks are on the market, including *EPC Climbing: A Climber's Guide to El Potrero Chico* (Frank Madden). El Potrero Chico Guides (802-922-4598; www.elpotrerochicoguides.com) leads climbers during the winter months.

▶ **Accommodations**: From camping to house rentals, PotreroChico.org provides an excellent overview of lodging options.

RED ROCK

RECOMMENDED BY **Phil Powers**

In 2018, more than forty-two million visitors flocked to Las Vegas—conventioneers, gamblers, gourmands, celebrity-stalkers, and more. Few likely realize that one of America's rock climbing treasures rests just a few miles west of the Strip.

"I began coming to Red Rock in the '80s, both for personal climbing and to teach National Outdoor Leadership School (NOLS) courses," Phil Powers recalled. "We'd camp for two or three weeks, teaching students how to climb and fitting in our own climbs when we could. There's every sort of climbing imaginable here, though Red Rock is especially known for its big walls and longer routes. Very few places have long routes like this; in some ways, it's the sandstone Yosemite. I remember camping at Oak Creek one night, sitting around the campfire. A younger fellow joined us and was talking about his adventures. Wild Iris near Landers, Wyoming, had been recently developed, and he was saying that it had America's best climbing. He was facing away from the escarpment. I remember looking over his shoulder at the Rainbow Wall and thinking, 'Wild Iris is nice, but it's nothing like this.'"

Red Rock Canyon National Conservation Area protects nearly two hundred thousand acres of the Mojave Desert, a mere fifteen miles west of Las Vegas. (Red Rock's multihued sandstone crags and canyons can be spied from higher perches along the Las Vegas Strip.) Some of the walls here climb to three thousand feet and are the site of challenging multiday ascents . . . though there are enough enjoyable single-pitch climbs to satisfy less ambitious climbers. Jerry Handren's 2016 guidebook identifies some 2,300 routes; a vast number of bouldering problems await as well, particularly in Black Velvet Canyon and Calico Basin. The area is accessible by a one-way road that loops thirteen miles through the rocks. Although many routes are near the road, some require an approach of up to two hours.

OPPOSITE:
Joel Dashnaw
contemplates
the next move
on Panty Raid;
it's hard to
believe that
Red Rock
is just a
stone's throw
from the bustle
of Las Vegas.

DESTINATION

27

Red Rock was not seriously explored as a climbing venue until the early 1970s, when a local fellow named Joe Herbst, fueled by climbing adventures in Yosemite, among other places, began working on the region's awesome walls. In his guidebook, Jerry Handren describes how Herbst sent two such walls on Mount Wilson's east face, Jubilant Song and Triassic Sands. Rainbow Wall, which Herbst referred to as the "Sandstone Halfdome," was next, with frequent climbing partner Larry Hamilton in tow. As Fitz Cahall has noted on the Outdoor Research website, their first effort was ill-fated—loose blocks on the early pitches left their ropes and haul bags in tatters at the base of the wall. The pair returned the following year and sent the climb, one thousand feet and fourteen pitches. Now rated 5.12, it is considered by many to be Red Rock's most classic climb. Word got out, and visitors began trickling in. By the early 1990s, it was firmly on the climbing map. For a time, the cavalcades of climbers descending on Red Rock threatened to damage the resource. But heightened scrutiny from the Bureau of Land Management—including the re-designation of Red Rock as a National Conservation Area—have helped preserve and protect the delicate desert landscape.

"When I'm at Red Rock, I enjoy getting on the bigger walls," Phil continued. "One of my favorites is the Brownstone Wall in Juniper Canyon. There's a six-pitch route called Black Dagger [5.8] that's a great climb. On the right side of Brownstone Wall is a route called Armatron [5.9]. I went up there with my wife and fifteen-year-old son, and we had some very good climbing. The beauty of this route is that you can walk down. You traverse over a ridge with beautiful views, and then drop down into a chimney and descend about one thousand feet. It's a shady, efficient, safe way to get down. Another great wall is Angel Food. One of my favorite routes there is Tunnel Vision [5.7]. It's five or six pitches, depending on how long you stretch your ropes. About two thirds of the way, you access a tunnel through the rock for 150 feet, enter a cave behind a giant buttress, and come out the other side. It's another route where you can descend without rappelling by scampering down nearby gullies.

"Black Velvet Canyon is a section of Red Rock that's not on the loop road. [It's accessed from outside of the conservation area.] Black Velvet has perhaps the best rock at Red Rock: dark, varnished sandstone, very crisp and solid, with beautiful edges. It's home to a number of wonderful routes, especially on the Black Velvet Wall. Epinephrine (1,600 feet, 5.9) is a test piece for those who are getting into big-wall climbing. It's thirteen or fifteen pitches with lots of chimneying—a very big day. With lots of other fine routes nearby, including Dream of Wild Turkeys and Sourmash, Velvet is a wonderful playground."

Some visiting climbers will set up shop at 13-Mile Campground. Others might opt to get a room on the west side of Las Vegas. "I like to get an early start, not just to beat the crowds but to enjoy the cool, morning part of the day," Phil added. "We're often done by midafternoon. You can be back in town in time for a shower and a nice dinner. It's pretty mellow on the west side of Vegas, but it's not hard to get to the Strip if you want to do the Vegas thing. Red Rock is one of the few great climbing destinations where you can combine outside adventure with cosmopolitan pursuits."

Even during temperate months, Red Rock can get pretty hot. But solace can often be found among the canyons. "The canyons have little microclimates," Phil said. "It could be 90 degrees as you're hiking in, but then you reach a place like Pine Creek Canyon, with ponderosa pines and a creek. Stepping off a classic climb like Dark Shadows [on the Mescalito formation], you can wash your face in a cool pool of water. That's an experience I relish."

PHIL POWERS is a lifelong climber who has made more than twenty-five expeditions to Alaska, South America, and the Karakoram Mountains. He made the first ascent of the eight-thousand-foot Washburn Face on Denali, the first ascent of Lukpilla Brakk's Western Edge in Pakistan (VI, 5.11, A3), and the first winter traverse of the Tetons' Cathedral Peaks in 1992. Phil has also climbed two eight-thousand-meter peaks—K2 and Gasherbrum II—without the aid of supplemental oxygen. He has served on the boards of both the Access Fund and the AMGA. He is the recipient of the American Mountain Foundation's VIIth Grade Award for climbing achievement; the AAC Mountaineering Fellowship Grant; the Mug's Stump Climbing Grant; and the Wilderness Education Association's Paul Petzoldt Award for Excellence in Outdoor Education (2007). Phil also received the American Alpine Club's highest award for service, the Heilprin Award, in 2012. The author of two books, *Wilderness Mountaineering* and *Expedition Planning*, Phil is the CEO of American Alpine Club and a co-owner of Jackson Hole Mountain Guides.

If You Go

▶ **Getting There:** Las Vegas is served by most major carriers; Red Rock is roughly fifteen miles west of the city.

▶ **Best Time to Visit**: Spring and fall are prime climbing times; south-facing walls can be tackled in the winter, weather permitting.

▶ **Level of Difficulty**: Though celebrated for its big walls, Red Rock has many single-pitch climbs, sport routes, and bouldering problems—something for almost everyone.

▶ **Guides**: A number of guides are available, including *Red Rocks: A Climber's Guide*, 2nd ed. (Jerry Handren). Several outfitters lead guided climbs here, including Jackson Hole Mountain Guides (800-239-7642; www.jhmg.com).

▶ **Accommodations**: 13-Mile Campground is the only campground in the National Conservation Area and does accept reservations (877-444-6777; www.recreation.gov). If you opt for a motel, look on the west side of Las Vegas (www.visitlasvegas.com).

DESTINATION

27

NORTH CONWAY

RECOMMENDED BY **Brad White**

Though he grew up in the Granite State, Brad White had never thought about climbing . . . until he visited North Conway on a ski trip in 1975. "I grew up in western New Hampshire and played a lot of team sports. I wasn't much of an outdoorsperson. After skiing one day near North Conway, I happened upon Cathedral Ledge, a five-hundred-foot-high granite cliff—literally seven minutes from downtown. I looked up and remember thinking, 'I don't think I'll ever climb this, but it's pretty impressive.' A little farther down the road, at the north end of Cathedral, there was an ice climbing area. I'd never even heard of ice climbing, but there were two guys doing it. I was fascinated. I came back into town and stopped at a new store, International Mountain Equipment. It had been in business a year, and the owner was Paul Ross, a celebrated English climber. I started looking at gear and was further intrigued. I walked up to Paul and said I wanted to learn to climb. He asked, 'Have you ever climbed before?' I said 'No.' He asked, 'Have you ever been a Boy Scout, know any knots?' I said, 'No.' He asked, 'Have any outdoor gear?' And I said, 'No.' And he said, 'Fine. We'll take you out next weekend.' I came back up and went ice climbing. I enjoyed it so much, I came back up in the summer and learned to rock climb with Ed Webster, who went on to write several guidebooks. I was his first rock climbing client! I moved here in 1977. And now I'm co-owner of the climbing school."

North Conway is on the eastern edge of New Hampshire, about eighty miles north of the state capital, Concord. It's bordered by the 750,000-plus-acre White Mountain National Forest to the north and west, and the state of Maine to the east. The town has been a popular outdoor retreat since the mid-nineteenth century, thanks largely to landscape painters—among them Thomas Cole, founder of the Hudson River School of painting—whose work captured the region's natural beauty and encouraged down-

country residents to make their way north. "What attracted me to move to North Conway was the accessibility of so many quality mountain experiences," Brad continued. "Some great rock climbing venues might have big walls to climb, but not much else. North Conway has the first-rate trad climbing, but there's also high-quality ice climbing, hiking, ski areas, backcountry skiing, mountain biking—all very nearby. Plus, you have hundreds of other cliffs throughout the White Mountains, including world-famous sport climbing at Rumney and the alpine playground of Mount Washington, just a bit farther away. In the spring, I can ski Tuckerman's Ravine in the morning and climb Cathedral Ledge in the afternoon. Depending on what the conditions are in a given season, I can work on different aspects of my outdoor skills. A heavy snow year, I'll do lots of skiing; a light snow year usually means good ice for climbing. If it's a rainy spring, I'll do aid climbing on overhanging cliffs. North Conway helps me to be as well rounded as I can possibly be."

There's a long history of rock climbing around North Conway, beginning in the 1920s; it's no surprise, then, that the region is a trad climbing stronghold. "You're not going to find a lot of sport climbing around here," Brad advised, "but for gear-based climbing, it's outstanding. Cathedral Ledge and Whitehorse Ledge are our poster children, standouts in the valley. One of the great beginner climbs is Upper Refuse [5.5]. It can be done in four short pitches. You hike down and around the side of the cliff. Once you're roped up, you've got immediate exposure—climb fifty feet, and suddenly there's two or three hundred below you. For some, it's the most incredible experience; for others, the most terrifying. You work your way up a ramp, and then there's a short pitch of about forty feet to the top. Then you step over a fence, and you're at the overlook area. There's a road that goes to the top, and when you get there, tourists will come over and ask two questions: Did you come up the front? How long did it take? It's quite a finish, going from a no-man's-land high on the wall to the overlook where people may crowd around you. Thin Air, at 5.6, is another classic. It goes up the center of a blank face over four pitches. It's relatively well protected, but provides outstanding exposure at the 5.6 level.

"If you climb at 5.9, a spectacular three-pitch route is Recompense, which goes right up the central buttress of Cathedral Ledge, up the edge of a formation called the Prow. The last pitch near the top has a big arching corner. The climb was put up by John Turner, who's known for doing a lot of bold stuff around here in the '50s and '60s. The first few times I climbed it, there were wooden wedges on the corner, with cords hanging through. My first thought was 'What the heck are these?' They're gone now. Climbing that route

OPPOSITE:
Cathedral Ledge
is home to
many of North
Conway's
great ascents,
including
Recombeast,
being tackled
here by
Sara Reeder.

DESTINATION

28

131

on a good day, I feel like I'm going strong, climbing well, and then I remember that fifty years ago these guys were doing it with wooden wedges. It checks your ego a bit. An even stouter climb is the Prow [5.11d], which is to the right of Recompense, and was first put up by Paul Ross and Hugh Thompson. It's well protected, over five or six short pitches. Again, there's incredible exposure, and the quality of rock is wonderful. The Conway granite is every bit as good as Yosemite granite. I read all the history of the route and worked for a long time to free-climb the Prow. When I finally did it, it was cool to feel part of the club that had free-climbed it."

Elvio's is a go-to spot for dinner and comparing notes. "The International Mountain Equipment store used to have part of the building walled off, and that's where the original Elvio's was located," Brad recalled. "People would gather in the store to discuss the day, and then get some pizza on the other side of the wall. Elvio's eventually got bumped out and is now down the street. People will still often stop in at IME before heading for pizza."

BRAD WHITE is an AMGA Certified Rock Instructor and is Avalanche Level Two Certified. He started climbing in 1975 at age twenty-one, with assistance from International Mountain Climbing School guides in North Conway. Brad was offered a chance to guide for IMCS in 1991, and he jumped in with both feet. Time off during off-seasons gave him the chance to explore the White Mountains even more, on rock, ice, and skis. By 1997, he had become VP/Head Guide and a partner in IMCS. Brad's travels—as a guide and on personal trips—have taken him across the American West and around the world, including Mont Blanc, Alaska; Nepal, Peru; and Pakistan. Today, Brad is president, director, and co-owner of IMCS. He lives in North Conway with his wife, Barbara, and has two beautiful children.

If You Go

▶ **Getting There:** North Conway is about one hundred miles from Manchester, New Hampshire, which is served by several carriers, including Southwest (800-435-9792; www.southwest.com).

► **Best Time to Visit**: The climbing season extends from mid-spring through fall, though fall offers the best conditions.

► **Level of Difficulty**: There are trad routes from 5.5 on up; beginners can successfully climb exposed cliffs with the help of a guide.

► **Guides**: *North Conway Rock Climbs* (Jerry Handren) is a go-to reference. Several outfitters provide guided climbs, including International Mountain Climbing School (603-356-7064; www.ime-usa.com/imcs).

► **Accommodations**: The Official North Conway New Hampshire Area Guide (www.northconwaynh.com) lists motel and camping options in the region.

THE SHAWANGUNKS

RECOMMENDED BY **Casey Chew**

For their convenience to a major urban area, their rare conglomerate of quartz and sandstone, and the unique contours of their rock faces, the Shawangunks—affectionately known as the "Gunks"—hold a special spot in many climbers' hearts.

 "My brother was sixteen months older than I, and he committed to rock climbing early on," Casey Chew recalled. "When he was in his early teens, he was investing his allowance in climbing gear. At age fifteen, he was doing trad climbing before I even knew what it was. But I became interested too. At the rock climbing gym we went to near Philadelphia, my brother was always talking to people to learn about hot spots. That's how he learned about the Gunks. Our parents would drive us up there before we had our licenses; it was a 3.5- or 4-hour drive from where we were in Pennsylvania. The first climb we did, I was shaking the whole time. I wasn't sure this was something I could enjoy. A week or so later, I realized how exciting that climb had been. By my mid-twenties, I had really embraced trad climbing. At the time I was living in New York City, studying comedy at Upright Citizens Brigade. I did a lot of weekend trips to the Gunks and was so stoked about it, I'd even make day trips. The quirky, small-town vibe of New Paltz, which is the hub for climbers, was a great complement to the climbing."

 The Shawangunk Ridge rests roughly eighty-five miles north of Manhattan, spread between Ulster, Sullivan, and Orange Counties. The surface rock here—Shawangunk Conglomerate—is underlaid by shale. Where the conglomerate is hard and resists weathering, the shale erodes, thus forming many cliffs and slopes—ideal for climbing. Most of the climbing areas fall under the purview of the Mohonk Preserve, a nonprofit land trust dedicated to protecting the northern Shawangunk Range for climbing and other outdoor activities.

OPPOSITE:
The "Gunks"
offer world-class
climbing just
a few hours
north of
Manhattan.

DESTINATION

29

The first recorded ascents of the Gunks date back to 1935 and are credited to Fritz Wiessner and Hans Kraus. A female climber named Bonnie Prudden also made her mark in those early days, making a number of first ascents, including the eponymous Bonnie's Roof. Climbers from far and wide began appearing at the Gunks in the '50s, and new routes were established. Among the most colorful visitors to arrive were a group that called themselves "the Vulgarians." The Vulgarians balked at the control the Appalachian Mountain Club exerted over access to the Gunks, and showed their disapproval by occasionally climbing in the nude. Most notable among the Vulgarians was Dick Williams, a gymnastic climber who pioneered many ascents in the 1960s, authored the first definitive guidebook for the region, and opened a climbing shop called Rock and Snow in New Paltz that's still in operation today.

There are some 1,200 routes at the Gunks, with most located in two cliff areas, the Trapps and the Near Trapps. Access for climbs at the Trapps is simplified by an adjacent carriage road. There's also the Grand Traverse Ledge that starts halfway up the cliff and follows much of the way. "You can do multi-pitch climbs or you can do one pitch and reach the ledge," Casey described. "When you're done with one climb, you can walk fifty yards left or right on the ledge to get to the next."

While you can certainly find climbs in the 5.12 and above range here, there are many less-taxing trad routes well suited for the less seasoned or adventurous climber. For Casey, High Exposure, a route first put up by Wiessner and Kraus in 1941, is a favorite. "It's one of the first routes I was taken up by my brother, and it's sentimental for that reason," he shared. "If I'm taking a newbie up to the Gunks, I'll lead them up High Exposure, no matter how long the line. It's not especially difficult, but the commitment you make when you pull out over the ledge is always a heady experience. Another more difficult climb that I like is the Yellow Wall [a 5.11c]. It's quite beautiful—it takes its name from the color of the lichen on its face, which has an orange and yellow tint. The colors give it a cool feng shui. It's a pretty straightforward, steep wall, though you're really exposed. It's a grunt fest. I'm also a fan of the roof pulls that are available, like Feast of Fools [5.10b]. It's super steep, almost ninety degrees, but there are good holds."

Whether you're preparing for a day on the cliffs or unwinding afterward, the town of New Paltz has you covered. "Mountain Harbor Deli has excellent breakfast sandwiches," Casey said. "Mexicali Blue is a fantastic burrito place. A favorite gathering spot is Mountain Brauhouse, which has a bunch of German beers on tap and bratwurst. If you need any gear, Rock and Snow is one of the coolest shops on the East Coast."

High Exposure was one of the first climbs that Casey completed with his brother. It would also be their last together. "My brother had brain cancer," Casey said. "The year before he passed, we went all over America with a trailer, climbing in the national parks. My brother was going toward longer and longer climbs before his body deteriorated. He was less interested in grades, more interested in seeing what his body was capable of. After he died, I took his ashes up to the Gunks. A buddy of mine who worked at Rock and Snow and I did a summit session on High Exposure. We started when it was still dark, and got to the top as the sun came up. We scattered his ashes at the top. I've climbed many harder ascents in my life, but that climb stands out: seeing the beautiful hills of the Hudson Valley, the circling hawks and buzzards, and finishing a classic climb, the first climb my brother took me up."

CASEY CHEW began climbing at a gym near Philadelphia when he was thirteen. Since that time, his climbing travels have taken him to many of America's national parks to various international destinations, including New Zealand . . . though the Gunks remain a sentimental favorite. Casey's passion for climbing has led him to work as an arborist, scaling large trees near his home in southeastern Pennsylvania.

If You Go

▶ **Getting There:** New Paltz/the Gunks are within a two-hour drive to New York City.

▶ **Best Time to Visit**: Spring and fall are prime climbing times; summers can be hot and humid. Fall foliage can be stunning.

▶ **Level of Difficulty**: There's a broad range of climbs at the Gunks to suit beginners and experts alike; there are also many bouldering problems.

▶ **Guides**: The Mohonk Preserve highlights a number of guide services at www.mohonk preserve.org/visit/activities/climb.html.

▶ **Accommodations**: The Samuel F. Pryor III Shawangunk Gateway Campground (www .mohonkpreserve.org/visit/camping.html) is a favorite of climbers. New Paltz has a number of chain hotels.

CASTLE HILL

RECOMMENDED BY **Timy Fairfield**

Timy Fairfield had always wanted to visit New Zealand. And that was before he'd even heard of Castle Hill.

"My mom visited New Zealand in the early '90s and said I'd have to go," Timy began. "I'd been intrigued by the country since I'd first seen imagery of rugby matches, the All Blacks doing the haka [a ceremonial Maori challenge that's performed before matches begin]. New Zealand was a far-off place with beaches and mountains and snow, all in a relatively small area—a very dynamic place. *Lord of the Rings* made an impression too. That's how many of us came to understand how beautiful the landscape was. I'd met climbers from New Zealand when I was competing, and knew there was rock there. Skiing, surfing, climbing—New Zealand has it all. But during my competitive climbing career, there were no major events held there, and I never made it.

"Back in 2008, one of my sponsors—Skins Clothing—wanted some fresh content and invited me to go to do a photo shoot. Within a month, I was in Christchurch. I was immediately struck by the natural light. It reminded me of my home in New Mexico, which is known for its brilliant light. Soon after I was off to Castle Hill."

Castle Hill lies about fifty miles northwest of Christchurch, along the scenic Arthur's Pass Highway. It's marked by the immense limestone boulders that dot the grazing lands here, in the shadow of the rugged Craigieburn Range to the west. Castle Hill was so named because early Anglo visitors thought the rocks resembled castle ruins, and most who've visited Castle Hill will come away feeling that the rocks have a special energy. The Dalai Lama was especially moved: The story goes that during a visit to Christchurch in 2002, his holiness sensed a negative energy in the city. He was taken to Castle Hill and was so overcome that he named the area a "spiritual center of the universe."

OPPOSITE:
Timy Fairfield pulls off a full points dyno at Castle Hill, a move that would be immortalized in his company's logo.

DESTINATION

(30)

139

"We arrived at Castle Hill in the New Zealand fall," Timy continued, "and conditions were a little tough. There was an early blast of winter—at first very humid, then rain, sleet, and wind. Still, we wanted to wander around and reflect. We'd go out on full-moon nights, in storms. The dramatic weather and light revealed the depths of the timelessness of the place. I liked Castle Hill's sense of desolation, almost like a desert place. The wind and sun are strong, harsh, like the desert. It's hard to have much outside contact, which is good for contemplation. It's a turbulent environment, and for me, this brings on dynamic thinking."

There are more than five thousand bouldering problems around Castle Hill, as well as a smaller number of sport climbs. Many are concentrated around three areas—Spittle Hill, Quantum Field, and Wuthering Heights. (Nearby Flock Hill also boasts extensive bouldering opportunities.) The climbing is particularly physical; as UKClimbing has noted, "a local jest is that wrestling sheep would be good training and they are not far from wrong." "The rocks are atypical, rather difficult to read," Timy described. "I found them very slopy, and the holds small. There are also large features that require gymnastic moves. I'd liken it to Fontainebleau but on limestone. The texture and beauty of the rock is amazing, inspiring for my work designing climbing gyms. The boulders are like a sculpture garden; there seemed to be a logic, a telos to them, almost like a natural Stonehenge. I didn't adapt to the rock all that well at first. But eventually I pulled off a full points dyno. We hadn't planned it, but the photographer who was along, Nathan Bancroft, caught the moment. The money shot from the trip later became the image from which our company's [Futurist Climbing] logo was designed by Ted Geving."

One of Timy's greatest Kiwi experiences was the realization of his earliest New Zealand fantasy—attending an All Blacks match in Christchurch. "On the drive from Castle Hill to Christchurch, there were so many rugby pitches, with boys and girls playing," Timy said. "They were like baseball fields in the Midwest. At the match, New Zealand destroyed England. It was refreshing to see the colonized country beat the motherland. Watching the All Blacks perform the haka, I was moved by how they embraced Maori culture. It got me stoked on New Zealand. After seeing how the country operates—celebrating its native people, pursuing a more sustainable path in its use of natural resources—I had hope for mankind."

TIMY FAIRFIELD is a professional rock climber. His career has been focused on competition, sport climbing, bouldering, and a commitment to proliferating rock climbing through his ongoing passionate practice of climbing, as well as by acting as a positive spokesperson for the sport. As a member of the U.S. National Climbing Team for over a decade, he participated in National, World Cup, International Open, and Invitational Masters–level events. Timy is one of the few climbers in the world to win national and international events in all three competition disciplines of the sport: bouldering, sport climbing, and speed climbing. Timy lived and trained with coaches in France for five years during his pursuit of international competition. His climbing career has enabled him to travel to more than forty countries throughout North and Central America, Europe, and Asia. Timy has visited and conducted business with hundreds of commercial climbing facilities worldwide. He has set routes for international competition in the United States, Europe, and Asia. In 2009, Timy established Futurist Climbing, which provides consulting and climbing-wall design services for climbing gyms. He lives in New Mexico with his wife.

If You Go

▶ **Getting There:** Castle Hill is 1.5 hours' drive from Christchurch, which is served by many carriers, including Air New Zealand (800-262-1234; www.airnewzealand.com).
▶ **Best Time to Visit**: Climbing is possible year-round. Though rain passes through, the rocks dry fairly quickly.
▶ **Level of Difficulty**: There's a bit for everyone here, though the surfaces will take some adjustment for most boulderers.
▶ **Guides**: *The Comprehensive Castle Hill Climbing Guide* (Matt Pierson and Alan Davison) is a good resource.
▶ **Accommodations**: There are several basic campgrounds nearby, including the Craigieburn shelter and Lake Pearson, both managed by the New Zealand Department of Conservation (www.doc.govt.nz). Flock Hill Lodge (+64 33188196; www.flockhill.co.nz) offers camping and simple lodging with more amenities.

WICHITA MOUNTAINS WILDLIFE REFUGE

RECOMMENDED BY **Adam Peters**

Oklahoma may not spring to mind when one is considering a climbing vacation, but Adam Peters may change your mind about that.

"The unique geology and topography in the southwestern part of Oklahoma makes it special," he began. "It's completely unlike what you might expect—wheat fields, cattle, and oil derricks. The Wichita Mountains region is reminiscent of places in Wyoming, granite outcroppings atop rolling hills covered with Indian grass. You don't even realize you're getting into the mountains until you're suddenly there. One moment you're in those wheat fields; the next, you're immersed in lush environs. The Wichitas speak to a certain type of climber; they're not going to appeal to most sport climbers or boulderers. There's a staunch ethic of trad climbing, and climbers there are proud of this tradition. For the first few years, I didn't even realize there was such a thing as sport climbing! The quality of the granite in the Wichitas is exceptional, as good as it gets in the United States. Another cool thing is that you're in a wildlife refuge, with free-range bison, elk, deer, and wild turkey roaming about. You could be belaying your partner and have a bull bison feeding twenty yards away."

The Wichita Mountains Wildlife Refuge encompasses nearly 60,000 acres in the southwestern corner of Oklahoma; 22,400 acres are open to public use. The refuge, an unspoiled landscape of oak forests and mixed grass prairies, is bifurcated by two ranges of granite mountains that run east to west. According to the Wichita Mountains Climbers Coalition, climbing in the refuge goes back to the 1940s, when an intrepid soul put up a first ascent of Great Expectations on Elk Slab. Since then, hundreds of routes have been established on Mount Scott, the Narrows, and Crab Eyes, among other sites; most are in the 5.6 to 5.11 range.

OPPOSITE:
In the
southwestern
corner of
Oklahoma,
the Wichitas
present an
unexpected
trad climbing
treat.

DESTINATION

31

There are a number of classics in the Wichitas for climbers of a variety of skill levels. Adam ticked off a few on his list. "Crazy Alice is an iconic 5.8 route in the middle of the Zoo Wall in the Narrows area. It's one of those test pieces when you're starting to feel comfortable with 5.8s. Mr. Clean is another good 5.8 on Lower Mount Scott. When you start moving into 5.9/5.10 territory, Foolish Behavior [5.9+] is a mega-classic. Moving further into the 5.10 zone, my favorite is probably Power Series, over in the Crab Eyes area of Charon's Gardens. It's on the East Face and is a really pretty formation—there are two giant boulders on top of an eighty-foot cliff. Another fine 5.10—really scary, but an amazing climb—is Dr. Coolhead, which is also on the Zoo Wall. When you break into the 5.11 and 5.12 class of routes, you'll want to tackle League of Doom [5.11c], which is on the Lichen Wall in the Narrows. It's one of the best routes I've ever done. If you haven't had enough once you're done, tackle a third pitch to reach the top, Spaceballs [5.11a]. Ra [5.11d], on the East Face of Crab Eyes, is a finger crack climb that's a great test piece for any aspiring hardman."

As mentioned above, there aren't many sport climbs in the refuge, but a few are noteworthy for Adam. "I like Repeat After Me [5.10c] on Lower Mount Scott," he opined. "Another great bolted route—one of the most classic sport climbs in the Wichitas—is Aerial Anticipation [5.11c], in the Narrows. Once you get to 5.12s, there aren't as many. The most standout for me is Rap Bolters from Hell [5.12a]. It's always my gage for what constitutes a 12a climb. When you're thinking of 5.13s, you have Tied to the Whipping Post [5.13a], on the Lost Dome Wall at Charon's Gardens."

When the day is done, there's little question where climbers will head for some grub. "The iconic place to hang out is Meers Store and Restaurant in the town of Meers," Adam shared. "Meers is almost a ghost town. All that's left is the restaurant. The Meersburger is the specialty. It's made from grass-fed longhorns that the owners raise, and comes on an aluminum pie plate. They also have amazing homemade cobblers, ice cream, and a wheat beer that's made for them. You can't visit the Wichitas without stopping for a Meersburger. If you want a break from climbing, I'd recommend visiting the Star House, which was the home built by Quanah Parker, the last of the Comanche chiefs. The Wichitas were his stomping grounds before the Indian Wars."

Almost every climbing trip involves a degree of exploration. Though Adam knows the region intimately, this principle still holds true when he returns to climb in the Wichitas. "Each time I go back, I find myself exploring who I am as a climber," he reminisced. "It's the place where I grew up in my climbing career. Being on the rock there, seeing the bison and elk in this unspoiled country, feels like going home."

ADAM PETERS is team and event specialist at Petzl America. Before joining Petzl, he served as a senior program manager and regional manager at American Alpine Club. An Oklahoma native, Adam has climbed extensively throughout North America and in Europe. Although he's gravitated toward steep, featured limestone sport routes, you can still find him plugging gear from time to time near his home in Salt Lake City, Utah, or on his yearly pilgrimage back to Oklahoma. He holds a juris doctor from Oklahoma City University School of Law and now calls Utah home.

If You Go

▶ **Getting There:** The Lawton-Fort Sill Airport is twenty-five miles from the Wichita Mountains Wildlife Refuge and is served by American Airlines (800-433-7300; www.aa .com). Oklahoma City is roughly ninety miles from the refuge and has service from most major carriers.

▶ **Best Time to Visit**: Spring and fall provide the best conditions, though climbing can be had year-round.

▶ **Level of Difficulty**: There's an abundance of intermediate terrain at the refuge, with some routes suited for beginners and experts.

▶ **Guides**: *Oklahoma Select: A Climber's Guide* (Tony Mayse) is a good reference. The Wichita Mountains Climbers Coalition (www.wichitamountains.org) also provides helpful information.

▶ **Accommodations**: There are several campgrounds nearby: Doris Campground is in the refuge with sites available on a first-come/first-served basis; and Lake Latonka (580-529-2663; www.lawtonok.gov), just outside the refuge. The Lawton Fort Sill Chamber of Commerce (580-355-3541; www.lawtonfortsillchamber.com) lists motel options in the area.

LION'S HEAD

RECOMMENDED BY **Greg Williamson**

Ontario, Canada's most populous province, was not dealt the best of hands in terms of mountains; the glaciers mostly took care of that. But what Ontario might be lacking in massifs it makes up for with the Niagara Escarpment. The escarpment, which stretches in a horseshoe shape from Watertown, New York, in the east to eastern Wisconsin in the west, includes some 450 miles of ridges in southern Ontario. Geologists estimate that the Niagara Escarpment dates back four hundred million years, to a time when the Great Lakes were a shallow, tropical sea. Much of the province's climbing terrain is found along the escarpment. And its little disputed crown jewel is found on a peninsula jutting into Lake Huron's Georgian Bay—Lion's Head.

OPPOSITE: Leslie Timms en route to a first ascent on Above the Clouds, a 5.13 trad/mix.

"Lion's Head is a beautiful combination of cliffs and water," Greg Williamson began. "The quality of the limestone is really good, especially compared with the rest of Ontario. You can hike the Bruce Trail [which rambles over five hundred miles, much of it following the Niagara Escarpment] and come upon other beautiful lakeside cliffs. But none have the same rock quality. It's kind of weird how the rock at Lion's Head formed to be so well suited for climbing. Typically, if you're trying to establish a new route, lots of cleaning is required. I developed routes at Lion's Head that didn't require any cleaning at all. The water in Georgian Bay certainly adds to the appeal of the place. It's a shade of blue that's out of some tropical dream destination—though it's certainly not tropical in its temperature! It's so clear, you can see fish swimming below when you're on the cliff."

Lion's Head rests on Isthmus Bay, midway up the east side of the Bruce Peninsula, a spit of land that separates Georgian Bay from the main basin of Lake Huron; it's about 160 miles north of Toronto. The peninsula is home to two of Ontario's national parks, Fathom Five National Marine Park (a haven for wreck divers) and Bruce Peninsula

DESTINATION

32

147

National Park, which safeguards the flora and fauna of this richly biodiverse region. The port village of Lion's Head takes its name from the shape of its limestone cliffs when viewed from the Bay. It's been a popular summer retreat for generations of canoeists, kayakers, and hikers tackling portions of the Bruce Trail. In recent years, it's seeing more and more climbers. "There's a group of twenty-five or thirty hard-core climbers who are passionate about the place and go there every weekend," Greg continued. "Summer weekends can get busy. But if you're willing to hike a little farther, you can find an area to yourself."

Development at Lion's Head began in earnest in the early 1990s, led at first by Dave and Reg Smart, Lohan Kaandorp, John Wier, Chris Oates, and Marc Bracken, and later by Gus Alexandropoulous, Daniel Martian, and Sonnie Trotter. Though few can argue with the incredible beauty of the place, not everyone is enamored with the Lion's Head climbing experience. "People either love it to death or don't like it at all," Greg explained. "The grades tend to be a bit hard. It's very exposed. And the logistics of climbing there turn some people away." The aforementioned logistics begin with a twenty-minute hike in to reach the cliffs. Next, you'll need to rappel down. "Climbing at Lion's Head is a serious undertaking," Greg noted in the introductory notes to his guidebook. "Climbers should be proficient at rappelling, ascending a fixed line, rigging hanging belays, and self-rescue." Greg notes that it is possible to access many of the routes without rappelling or hanging belays by hiking a bit farther to Stinger Gulley and scrambling down, though you'll need to bushwhack your way back to some of the ascents.

Most of the routes at Lion's Head are single-pitch sport climbs, and Greg has developed a number of them. "I like developing new routes," he said, "but there's not a lot of rock left now to work with. My friends developed a lot of the original lines. I've tried to add in around the edges. The predominant grades here are 5.10/5.11; there are so many good climbs in that range. One is Maneline [5.10a]. It's on the biggest sector of the cliff [Maneline Wall], and it's really long for a single pitch, at least one hundred feet. The rock is good all the way and pretty similar in difficulty, consistent to the grade. It's hard to go wrong with Maneline. Right nearby is Nimbus [5.10a]. It's not as long as Maneline but has a great setting and is very exposed. Going up in grade is I Wonder Where the Lions Are [5.12a]. The rock is impeccable. It's a four-star climb for Lion's Head; it would be a four-star route in Spain or France too. Among the harder climbs is Maxi Pista [5.13c]. It's a really long, really varied climb with several uniquely difficult cruxes. If you're a newcomer to Lion's Head, doing four or five pitches would be a pretty big day. Time gets eaten up quickly by all the logistics of climbing here." The campgrounds at Lion's Head Beach and White Bluff are home for visiting campers . . . with perhaps a stop en route for a libation at Rachel's or the Lion's Head Inn. (White Bluff, it should be added, has some excellent sport climbing as well.)

The cliffs at Lion's Head face the northwest. On warm summer days, climbers can enjoy relative shade until early afternoon. In the early evening, they can revel in the last hour of light. "When the sun starts going down, it's the golden hour at Lion's Head," Greg mused. "There's something about the light. The water becomes a deeper blue, the trees a greener green, and the cliffs turn orange. It never gets old."

GREG WILLIAMSON has climbed his whole adult life at Lion's Head, and helped establish many routes there . . . and once rope-soloed sixty routes (up to 5.12+) in a single day. In an earlier life, he was a competitive bodybuilder and super-bike moto-racer. Now, Greg is an architect specializing in residential designs, and lives near Lion's Head with his wife and children.

If You Go

▶ **Getting There:** Lion's Head is roughly 160 miles from Toronto and 240 miles from Detroit, both of which are served by most major carriers.

▶ **Best Time to Visit**: June through September is the main climbing season.

▶ **Level of Difficulty**: A majority of the climbs at Lion's Head are rated 5.10 and above; this, combined with the challenges accessing the crags, makes it best for climbers of at least intermediate ability.

▶ **Guides**: There are several guidebooks available, including *Ontario Rock Climbing: The Best of Southern Ontario* (Jesse Wong), which incorporates Greg Williamson's work on Lion's Head.

▶ **Accommodations**: Lion's Head Tourism (www.visitlionshead.ca) highlights lodging options, including campgrounds.

SMITH ROCK

RECOMMENDED BY **Jim Ablao**

Hundreds of thousands of vacationers from the Portland area circle Mount Hood en route to the destination resorts of central Oregon near Bend and Sunriver. Coursing through the high desert near the small town of Terrebonne, they may notice a curious amalgamation of rocks to the east. Those who slow down a bit may note that one formation somewhat resembles the face of a monkey. Most will not realize that this is the birthplace of American sport climbing—Smith Rock.

"Smith Rock presents a gorgeous canyon with awesome tuff," Jim Ablao began. "It's one of the most aesthetic climbing spots in Oregon. There was some trad climbing here in the '30, '40s, and '50s, but it really began to boom in the '80s with the introduction of sport climbing. It opened up a whole new style in the United States, parallel to what was going on in France at the time. When U.S. climbers saw rock stars from Europe coming to Smith Rock and sport climbing here, it got them to look at sport climbing in a whole new light. And many began embracing the style. Smith Rock offers incredible convenience and accessibility. It's only a twenty-minute drive from Bend; once you're there, it's only a fifteen-minute hike to a tremendous amount of climbing. Initially, it was the very hard routes that drew people here. Now, I think Smith Rock is recognized for its many moderate routes. It's very accessible to weekend warriors—there are some amazing climbs in reach of intermediate climbers. And there are still new climbs to be pioneered."

Smith Rock State Park sits near the geographic center of Oregon, some twenty miles east of the Cascade Mountains. The formation here juts from the rugged high desert terrain to heights approaching six hundred feet. Like so much of the geology in this part of the world, Smith Rock has a volcanic provenance; climbers will find a combination of welded tuff and basalt that's been further shaped by the Crooked River, which courses

OPPOSITE:
Chris Sharma
works on Just
Do It, a 5.14c
on Monkey
Face—one of
Smith Rock's
ultimate
test pieces.

DESTINATION

33

through the park, a pleasing (and, in the summer, cooling) ribbon of blue. The park is home to more than two thousand routes, all compressed into twelve areas spread across a compact 650 acres. It was one of those routes—Chain Reaction (5.12)—that ushered in a whole new era of American climbing, thanks to a young man named Alan Watts. Watts's father, Jack, was one of the early pioneers at Smith Rock in the 1950s, putting up a number of routes with his friends Jim and Jerry Ramsey. (Smith Rock's first recorded climb is credited to Johnny Bissell, in 1935.) Alan began climbing at Smith Rock when he was fourteen; by his own assessment, he wasn't very good until he reached his early twenties.

By 1982, Alan had climbed all of the established routes and had begun exploring interesting lines by rappelling down them. While dropping down he'd drill bolts, a technique he referred to as "rap bolting." When SmithRock.com asked Watts what inspired him to start putting up routes in this manner, he said there were two reasons: "Part of it was just out of necessity to do the more appealing lines. The other reason was that it was just easier. Going from the ground up, doing routes that way, was pretty scary! Part of it was just being a wimp, when it came down to it. But routes that we could climb from the ground up were becoming few and far between." It was in February 1983 that Watts first tackled Chain Reaction from *below*—an achievement that many recognize as the first recorded sport climb. (When the route appeared on the cover of *Mountain* magazine in 1986, the world saw what Oregon had to offer . . . and a new destination was born.)

For elite climbers, it was two routes that put Smith Rock on the map. One was To Bolt Or Not To Be (5.14a), the first climb of its class to be put up in North America (by French climber Jean-Baptiste Tribout in 1986). As MountainProject.com has noted, the list of climbers "who've ticked this wall reads like a who's who of free climbing." The other is Just Do It, a 5.14c route on Monkey Face. "Monkey Face is a 350-foot spire that has the likeness near the top of a monkey, like Curious George," Jim said. "While most climbers will never conquer Just Do It, there are routes that can get intermediates to the top. And there are plenty of other routes that are well suited to less seasoned climbers. Though we're known for sport climbing, there are some fine trad climbs too. Most are single-pitch and within one hundred feet, with nice pockets and holes, very accessible for intermediates."

Jim described an average day at Smith Rock: "Many climbers like to start or end their day at Redpoint Climbers Supply in Terrebonne. They have coffee in the morning and tap beer for afterward—plus you can buy any supplies you might need. The Sunspot, a little diner, is a staple for breakfast. Once you get to the parking area, most crags are ten to twenty-five minutes' walk. If I'm guiding, I should be able to get people up four to eight routes in a day, in different parts of the park. When the day is done, there are some good options in Terrebonne. Basecamp has great pizza. The Depot offers fine dining, and its back porch has a view of Smith Rock. If you're looking for more options, Bend is just twenty minutes down the road."

JIM ABLAO has been guiding throughout the western United States since 1989 and has been a climbing guide at Smith Rock State Park since 1999. Over the years he has earned certification as an AMGA Rock Instructor and Rock Guide, and is also an AMGA Single Pitch Instructor Program Provider, SPI Provider Trainer, and AMGA Climbing Wall Instructor Program Provider. Jim's climbing has taken him to the summits and cliffs of Argentina, Chile, South Korea, Mexico, and Canada. He has taught and guided diverse terrain with many schools and programs including twelve years with the Colorado Outward Bound School, six years as a guide manager, and many years with various "youth at risk" and therapeutic programs. Jim lives in Bend with his wife and two daughters.

If You Go

▶ **Getting There:** Visitors can fly into nearby Redmond, Oregon, which is served by several airlines, including Alaska (800-252-7522; www.alaskaair.com). Portland, which is served by most major carriers, is a three-hour drive.

▶ **Best Time to Visit**: Spring and fall offer the best conditions, though with the high desert's dry climate, climbing can be had year-round.

▶ **Level of Difficulty**: There's an incredibly broad range of climbs here, both sport and trad.

▶ **Guides**: There are a number of outfitters that guide at Smith Rock, including Chockstone Climbing Guides (541-318-7170; https://chockstoneclimbing.com). *Rock Climbing Smith Rock State Park* (by Alan Watts) provides a great primer.

▶ **Accommodations**: Bivouac (or Bivy) Campground (541-548-7501) is popular with visiting climbers. SmithRock.com highlights local lodging and provides abundant information about the region.

BLED

RECOMMENDED BY **Matevz Vukotic**

If you're hoping to explore a place with a rich mountaineering culture, a dynamic history, and some excellent climbing opportunities, you could do much worse than Slovenia. "One of the things that makes Slovenia a great climbing venue is that it's such a small country and so diverse in its geography," Matevz Vukotic began. "In the same day, you can be on top of Mount Triglav at over nine thousand feet and exploring limestone at sea level on the Adriatic coast at a place like Osp. In the Bled region, there are three well-established climbing areas. Within two to two and half hours, you can drive almost anywhere in the country; there are more than ninety-five climbing areas with five thousand sport climbing routes to explore. You can climb for weeks and never be bored. And since Bled has so many other great outdoor amenities—rafting, kayaking, fly fishing, cycling, hiking, sightseeing—there's something for nonclimbers or for your days off."

OPPOSITE:
A bounty of sport
climbs awaits you
near the beautiful
city of Bled in
Gorenjska.

Slovenia is a republic whose identity—let alone location—may be little known to North Americans. Once annexed under the republic of Yugoslavia, the small mountainous nation is on the Balkan Peninsula, bordered by Austria to the north, Hungary to the northeast, Croatia to the south and southeast, and Italy and the Adriatic Sea to the west. Geographically centered between eastern and western Europe, Slovenia strikes a happy blend of the Italian, Austrian, and Slavic cultures that have come to bear upon it. The limestone peaks of the Julian Alps that dominate much of northwestern Slovenia are an extension of the central European Alps; a large portion of the range is contained by Triglav National Park, which comprises over 3 percent of the country's landmass and is adjacent to Bled.

It's hard to overstate the significance of Mount Triglav for Slovenians. During Slovenia's annexation, the mountain was a symbol of rebellion as Slovenians struggled

DESTINATION

34

for liberation. Once Yugoslavia dissolved and Slovenia became an independent nation, it emblemized the country's newfound sovereignty. A silhouette of Triglav is the center-piece of the Slovenian flag, and decorates the 50 euro cent coin. Picking up on this symbol of national solidarity, the first president of Slovenia, Milan Kučan, pronounced that it is the obligation of every Slovenian to climb Triglav at least once. Slovenia's passion for mountains has produced a remarkable number of notable climbers for a country of just over two million people. Past luminaries include Pavla Jesih, Dana Kuraltova, Tomaz Humar, and Silvo Karo; current stars include Janja Garnbret, Mina Marković, Domen Škofic, Marjan Manfreda, and Gregor Vezonik.

A crag called Bohinjska Bela is the go-to spot for climbers around Bled. "It's just five minutes from Bled by car," Matevz continued. "It began getting bolted in the early '90s and now has seventy-nine routes. [Much of the work was completed by Srečo Rehberger, who also established many routes in Mišja Peč.] The limestone there gives you many different sorts of holds—pinch, crimps—you can really polish your technique and build your finger strength. There are routes for almost everyone, from children and seniors to more skilled climbers; grades range from 5.3 to 5.14c. There may not be much here to interest a climber like Adam Ondra, but for beginners and intermediates, there's plenty. When you get to a decent height, there's beautiful scenery down the valley to the Sava Bohinjka River. If it's a warm summer day and you want to cool off, beautiful Lake Bled is nearby.

For those interested in climbing Mount Triglav, there are several ways to reach the top. Although there are a number of hiking trails to the summit (with via ferrata for steeper pitched sections), climbers tend to gravitate toward the North Face—a one-thousand-meter-tall, three-thousand-meter-wide wall of limestone. "The Slovenian route is the easiest way to the top," Matevz described. "There's some climbing, but it's mostly hiking. The German route is one of the more challenging ways to the summit. The hardest pitch is grade 4+. It's one of the highest walls in Europe. Most people don't realize that you can do such a big climb in Slovenia."

Whether you tackle Mount Triglav or busy yourself with the crags at Bohinjska Bela, you'll want to reward yourself with a slice of *kremna rezina*, also known as Bled cream cake. The confection—a magical concoction of custard, whipped cream, and puff pastry—dates back to 1953, when it was first served at Bled's Park Hotel. Having gained a protected designation of origin status, *kremna rezina* is available only in Bled.

Matevz Vukotic is a certified IFMGA mountain guide and canyoning guide based in Bled. He started rock climbing at the age of five, and by age twelve, had sent a multi-pitch climb on a 350-meter wall. Matevz soon began competing in ice climbing world cups, and later in skydiving junior world cups; in 2008, he became the world champion at the UIAA Ice Climbing Overall Ranking in speed ice climbing. His climbing adventures have taken him to Peru, South Korea, Switzerland, France, and Italy. Matevz is credited with the first winter ascent on Sphinx, the most difficult route on the North Face of Mount Triglav. He also garnered first place for male climbers at the IFMGA International Mountain Guide Climbing Championship in 2017. Matevz now operates Altitude Activities, a guiding company in Bled, with his twin brother.

If You Go

▶ **Getting There:** Fly into the capital city of Ljubljana, which is served by many airlines, including Air France (800-237-2747; www.airfrance.com) and Lufthansa (800-399-5838; www.lufthansa.com). From there, it's a roughly forty-minute drive to Bled.

▶ **Best Time to Visit**: May through October sees the best conditions; summer can be a bit crowded.

▶ **Level of Difficulty**: There's plenty of great terrain for beginner and intermediate climbers (with many routes between 5.10 and 5.12); experts will not find as much challenge around Bled, with the exception of the German route.

▶ **Guides**: Several guidebooks are available, including *Slovenia Sport Climbing Guidebook* (Sidarta; www.sidarta.si/en/product/slovenia-climbing-guide-en/). Altitude Activities (+386 70138811; www.altitude-activities.com) leads sport climbing trips around Bled and ascents of Mount Triglav.

▶ **Accommodations**: The Bled tourism website (www.bled.si/en) outlines lodging options.

ROCKLANDS

RECOMMENDED BY **Scott Noy**

For Scott Noy, it's a combination of factors that make Rocklands a very special place. "Fontainebleau may have more interesting movement, but what makes Rocklands the best place to go are the other things that fill out the package. The weather is perfect—dry and cold. The landscape is grand—weird, rocky, hilly—in a way that is reminiscent of the moon. There's one *S* bend before you enter; whenever I pass it, I feel I've passed the point of civilization, and experience a great sense of freedom. The road snakes through boulders, which seem endless; everyone I speak to says that the first time they drove up, their jaw dropped when they saw so much rock. When you're not climbing, the locals are friendly, and the food and wine are delicious. Some people who visit are happiest to tick off certain established problems on their list."

Rocklands rests roughly 150 miles north of Cape Town, in the Cederberg Mountains of the Western Cape. It's part of the Cape Floral Kingdom, which is celebrated for its rich diversity of plant life, perhaps best expressed in early September when the hillsides are festooned with wildflowers. Although the region is not as rich in wildlife as the game preserves of northeastern South Africa, it is home to interesting fauna. "The most common large animals you'll see are baboons," Scott continued. "They're about the size of a ten-year-old child; they used to steal our food when we camped. You'll also see antelope and a number of bird and snake species. Since it's essentially a desert, many animals are most active at night. Nocturnal creatures include aardvark and porcupine, among others." The Rocklands region was once the domain of the San people (also known as Bushmen), hunter-gatherers who roamed across southern Africa. Although the San are no longer present, their pictographs adorn certain rock faces in the region.

OPPOSITE:
Oddly enough,
the name
Rocklands does
not come from
the abundance
of boulders,
but an old
topographical
map.

DESTINATION

35

159

The fine grain sandstone boulders of Rocklands were revealed to the climbing world thanks to the sport climbing routes in the Cederberg. American climber Todd Skinner came upon the boulders of Pakhuis Pass in the 1990s and immediately recognized the potential. Skinner reached out to renowned boulderer Fred Nicole, who soon established a number of problems in the Roadside area of Rocklands. Since that time, countless others have contributed first ascents, making Rocklands one of the most prolific bouldering areas in the world. "People are often surprised to learn that climbers didn't come up with the name 'Rocklands,' Scott added. "It was called 'Rocklands' on the topographical map, which I guess speaks for itself."

There are so many problems around Rocklands—some 2,500 are recorded in the most recent edition of Scott's guidebook—that it's difficult to know where to begin. Scott shared a few that he enjoys. "I tend to gravitate toward aesthetic lines, as opposed to random holds on a wall. Linear lines, a crack, a groove, an arête that captures my attention. Sometimes you can walk up to a boulder and immediately feel like you have to climb it. Splash of Red (V10) is one of those beautiful lines. Cedar Spine (V9), another tall arête, is quite inspiring. A funny little line that I find unique in the 8 Day Rain section [so named because its climbing pioneers once had to hunker down for eight days to wait out a storm before they could climb] is called Chinese Food and Chocolate Pudding. It's an intermediate problem, not especially hard, but it requires unique moves—you have to use both of your thumbs. We've tried other ways, but it's the easiest way of doing it." Though there are a number of absurdly challenging problems at Rocklands (including Livin' Large, a V16 put up by Nalle Hukkataival in 2009), less seasoned boulderers will find plenty of more modest routes. One can also find many fine crags for sport climbing; after all, that's what first brought climbers here.

In the early days of Rocklands, the infrastructure was fairly limited. "There were really no established places besides this abandoned campsite," Scott recalled. Slowly the farmers cottoned to the idea that they could make some extra money by renting cottages to climbers. There was no guidebook then, just some word of mouth and a few hand-drawn topos. It was simple in those days—we'd just go out and explore, then come back in the evening and chat about it around a braai (barbecue). The wine there is fantastic, from both the Cederberg Mountains and the Stellenbosch region." Today, visiting climbers have a few good camping or lodging options, including De Pakhuys, Travellers Rest, and Alpha Excelsior.

DESTINATION

35

The sense of possibility and the chance for exploration that Rocklands affords has been perhaps its greatest appeal for Scott. "I've always been an explorer," he mused. "I like to see what's on the other side of the hill. Rocklands is such a huge area; over the years I've divided my time equally between established places and those off the beaten path. For me, climbing is not all about performance. It's about experiencing something new, something to share with others."

SCOTT NOY grew up on a farm in the Winelands of the Western Cape. While completing a sport science degree at Stellenbosch University, he was introduced to climbing by some fellow students. Initially, Scott focused his attention on the granite domes of Paarl Rock, which loomed large above his house; that led to him authoring the first complete climbing guide to the area. Soon he was introduced to Rocklands, where he found not only his love for bouldering but his second home and favorite place on earth as well. With the help of the international climbers who developed the areas, his buddies who spent months on end with him at camp, and the farmers who opened up their land, Scott juggled life and his studies (including a Medical Honours degree at University of Cape Town) to write a guide worthy of Rocklands, *Rocklands Bouldering*.

If You Go

▶ **Getting There:** Rocklands is 150 miles (roughly three hours) north of Cape Town. The nearest town is Clanwilliam.

▶ **Best Time to Visit**: Conditions are best from May through September, with July being the peak month.

▶ **Level of Difficulty**: With more than 2,500 routes, there's something for every boulderer at Rocklands.

▶ **Guides**: The definitive resource is *Rocklands Bouldering*, 2nd ed. (Scott Noy).

▶ **Accommodations**: De Pakhuys Farm (+27 836041459; www.depakhuys.com) and Kliphuis (+27 214830190; www.capenature.co.za) offer both camping and simple cottages.

DESTINATION

35

GYEONGGI-DO/JEJU

RECOMMENDED BY **John Burgman**

It's been said that 70 percent of South Korea is made up of mountains. "I'm not sure where people get that statistic from," John Burgman ventured, "but I think it could be true. Wherever I've been in the country, I'm either on a mountain or can see one. And it seems that most have been developed with climbing routes. There are more than four thousand routes in the country now, most on sturdy granite, and all easily accessible. Although South Korea is a very mountainous country, it's also home to some of the world's densest urban areas. Korean society values health and fitness; it seems that the density of the cities makes them conducive to little hole-in-the-wall climbing and bouldering gyms. Given the proximity of the mountains to the cities and the many gyms, you have so many options. You're left wondering, 'Where do I begin?'"

Climbing might not be the first thing to come to mind when one thinks of South Korea, what with its high-tech success stories and high-quality education system. But the truth is, climbing has become hugely popular in recent years, undoubtedly thanks in part to that booming tech industry—and all the extra disposable income its workers have to spend on leisure activities. Another factor that's contributed to climbing's spike in popularity is the success of the competitive climber Jain Kim. Her many victories have been well documented in Korean media, raising public awareness of rock climbing. Perhaps the most important factor that's led to climbing's growth in Korea is the social opportunities the sport provides—especially in gym settings. "Korea has a very strong grounding in Confucianism," John continued, "and Confucianism places great importance on the collective—the group rather than the individual. You see this everywhere—bath houses, karaoke bars, restaurants. There are always large groups together. This collectivism extends to sports. Where American climbers might have a partner or two, Korean climbers

OPPOSITE:
The city of Seoul is in view from some routes at Bukhansan, one of South Korea's most popular climbing spots.

DESTINATION

36

will have a crew. It's very formalized. They'll make flags and T-shirts with the name of their crew, and keep social media accounts for their crew. If you're lucky enough to be brought in, you're no longer just a climber, but an active participant in a social entity. It's like a second family that's devoted to having fun while climbing."

Most international adventures to South Korea will begin in Seoul. This works out well, as there's some great climbing to be found in Gyeonggi-do Province. "If you're willing to travel an hour or two, you can climb around Seoul for weeks," John enthused. "The most famous mountain—and one that's just north of Seoul—is Bukhansan. Bukhansan is unique for Korea, as many of its routes are multi-pitch. But be forewarned—Bukhansan is the most popular outdoor area near Seoul, and you will see crowds. I prefer two other areas that are an hour and a half outside of Seoul: Jobisan and Namhansan. At Jobisan, you're climbing these great wedges of granite. You'll be walking through the forest and will suddenly come to this expanse of rock. You'll be blown away by the quality of the stone. At Namhansan, dirt paths lead you through the forest past Buddhist statues and other religious iconography. You feel like you're traveling to a hallowed place, not just going climbing. You lose yourself in it, and then all of the sudden the path opens up to this huge crag and you remember, 'Oh yeah, I'm on a climbing trip.' There are about twenty routes, with some shallow roof sections that you need to climb over. It's never too overhanging, but physical enough. You earn those cold beers back in the city."

Jeju can feel a world away from Gyeonggi-do, though it is only an hour's flight south. "It's an island of wonderful quirks," John described, "totally different from anywhere else in Korea, with palm trees, beach huts, seaside coffee shops. It's a place made for curious exploration. Jeju is volcanic in makeup, and climbing is not on mountain faces, but on the stony banks of dried-out riverbeds. They're all single pitch; you're climbing up from the riverbeds. There's also great bouldering in many of the riverbeds. You just follow the riverbed along until you come to something interesting."

Hard or breakthrough climbs are not the only narratives of a great climbing experience. As John notes, sometimes the best parts of a climbing trip are the parts that weren't planned at all. "One time when I first got to Jeju, I connected with a friend to go bouldering," he recalled. "I was eager to find some challenging routes to test myself. We had our crash pads, and set off down a riverbed looking for some good stuff to climb. We found some spots that people had told us about, but pretty soon we slipped into looking for our own problems. Eventually we ended up at a puddle that was swimming with hundreds of

Oriental fire-bellied toads. They're just an inch or two long, with green backs and bright orange bellies. We were mesmerized. Then my friend shared some kimbap she'd made, a kind of seaweed and rice roll that's popular as a snack food. Soon after, we were napping on our crash pads. As the sun was going down, we woke up and hiked back out.

"I found this all amusing. I'd set out that morning planning to find something hard and climb it. Instead, we made up our own routes, came upon some frogs, had some homemade snacks and a great nap. It's not an epic tale, but it was spontaneous. I think the Korean climbing landscape is a wonderful entrée into such spontaneity."

JOHN BURGMAN is the author of *Island Solitaire* (based on his adventures in South Korea) and *Why We Climb: A Dirtbag's Quest for Vertical Reason.* He is currently writing a book on the history of competition climbing. He is also a former editor at *Outdoor Life* magazine and a Fulbright journalism grant recipient. His writing has appeared online or in print at *Climbing, Esquire, Gym Climber, The Rumpus, Portland Review,* and other outlets. John's climbing and camping adventures have taken him around the world, but he recently settled in Boulder, Colorado.

If You Go

▶ **Getting There:** Seoul is served by most major carriers. A number of domestic carriers serve Jeju.

▶ **Best Time to Visit**: Though there can be good conditions in the spring and summer, fall is generally best—with the added benefit of superb foliage.

▶ **Level of Difficulty**: Both Gyeonggi-do and Jeju offer a variety of climbing options, though big-wall aficionados will find the abundance of single-pitch climbs a bit lacking.

▶ **Guides**: John suggests visiting Korean Facebook groups like Seoul Climbers to gather information . . . or, better yet, visit a few climbing gyms in Seoul (there are nearly fifty) and chat up climbers (most can speak English).

▶ **Accommodations**: Korea has many guesthouses (comparable to hostels) that are well suited to budget travelers. www.guesthouseinseoul.org is a starting point for such lodging in Seoul; www.guesthouseinjejuisland.com in Jeju.

IBIZA

RECOMMENDED BY **Matt Samet**

Some may have the perception that the life of a climbing-magazine editor involves end-less free trips, wining and dining with equipment executives, and opportunities to kick back with Chris Sharma and other luminaries. In reality, an editor spends a lot more time massaging prickly prose into passable English, hunting down archival photo credits, and finding clever ways to squeeze one-thousand-word stories into five-hundred-word slots. But occasionally, as Matt Samet explained, there are some advantages.

"A photographer named Dave Munilla sent in a climbing guidebook [that he'd written with Toni Bonet] about Ibiza for potential review. My wife and I had just gotten married, and we were both working at *Climbing*. We wanted to go to Spain and I had already been to Mallorca, so we decided to try Ibiza. We couldn't go on our honeymoon right away due to deadlines, but we went in September 2009. Since the summer had passed, we thought that the club scene might have wound down a little—Ibiza is known a bit in the climbing world, but it's much more known for its super clubs. But that wasn't the case. There were still guys in tight shirts and women in miniskirts clomping around the streets, drunk. We were in bed by ten each night; we'd hear the drunks coming back at three or four, stum-bling up the stairs, puking over the balconies, etc. They were clearly not climbers. When you get away from the two main cities—Eivissa and Sant Antoni—it's all olive groves, vineyards, red-clay soil, sandy beaches, and limestone. The isolation at the cliffs was quite a contrast to the party scene in town. You pretty much have the rock to yourself."

Ibiza—known by some as the "White Island"—is the smallest (at 220 square miles) of the four Balearic Islands (Mallorca, Ibiza, Formentera, and Menorca) and rests about one hundred miles east of Valencia. Tourism came a bit slower to Ibiza than neighboring Mallorca, beginning with flower children who arrived to take in the idyllic surroundings

OPPOSITE: Ibiza may be better known for its nightlife than its climbing, but many gems await those willing to explore.

DESTINATION

37

in the 1960s. Nightclubs began springing up in the '70s, and jet-setters began arriving in the '80s, attracted by the island's laid-back vibe and a burgeoning after-hours party scene. As reported by the *Guardian*, it was Ibiza's eclectic "Balearic beat" that provided inspiration for a young DJ named Paul Oakenfold, who put his own spin on the music, giving birth to a genre now known as Acid House. Its popularity in England, fueled by copious amounts of MDMA, or ecstasy, brought greater notoriety to Ibiza. Today, the island draws all-star deejays from around the world, and during the summer, the party never seems to stop.

Sport climbing came to Ibiza in the late 1980s, as the party scene was reaching its fever pitch. In a story in *Climbing*, Matt identified the island's first sport climb as the four-pitch *Vidas Ejemplares* (5.9) situated at Buda, the island's tallest cliff near its southwestern corner. Now there are more than four hundred bolted routes scattered over a dozen areas. Though the greatest concentration of climbing cliffs is in Ibiza's north, spread along U-shaped bays (*calas* in local parlance), Buda is the largest single area by far, with more than 140 routes. "Ibiza is all limestone," Matt continued, "typically steep, with a fair bit of overhanging rock. It features tufas, extruded pillars, and lots of interesting columns—with three-dimensional shapes you can climb on, like stalactites. Most approaches take some time and involve descending seaward along piney, obscure tracks. Some of the standout crags are Punta Aubarca, Cueva de Egagrópilas, Santa Agnés, and Sol y Sombra." (It's worth noting that Matt has described Ibiza as an *adventure* sport-climbing destination, as the approaches are rugged and difficult to locate, and—at least as of 2009—some of the original bolts have corroded in the marine environment, creating dangerous conditions . . . though the bolts on more established routes have been updated.)

Cueva de Egagrópilas offered up an especially memorable experience. "It's a huge limestone cave, the size of St. Peter's Basilica, out on the Cap des Rubió peninsula," Matt described. "You park on this road surrounded by pine trees, rosemary, and Mediterranean cactus, and then you walk through the pines toward the sea. You wouldn't even know the rock was out there. In fact, the first time we went, we hiked too low, down along the waterline. When we looked up, the Cueva was there. It's this huge hole, filled with fourteen mega-pitches on stalactites, ranging from 5.11c to 5.13d. One of the climbs, Aroma de Archidona [5.13a/b], is a 110-foot run out of the cave's guts. No hold is smaller than a double-pad incut, and at the end, the angle is an unrelenting 125 degrees. It's a very wild spot with no development, just you and the cliffs and the sea—pretty magical. For the grade, this could be the best climb on the planet."

Coastal weather can always be a bit unpredictable, especially if you're on an island in the middle of the Mediterranean. Sometimes this uncertainty can lead to unexpected discoveries. "There was a day when we were planning to climb on the north side of Ibiza, but we got rained out," Matt recalled. "If the weather is bad in Colorado where I live, it's usually bad for some distance. But on Ibiza, if it's raining on one side, it could be sunny on the other. We headed south to Buda and were able to salvage the day. Buda is a huge escarpment looking out over the sea, gray and white limestone with slabs and bellies. I remember being so happy to be dry and climbing in such a beautiful spot."

MATT SAMET is an avid rock climber and the editor of *Climbing* magazine, based in Boulder, Colorado. He has been climbing for thirty-plus years. Matt is the author of *Climbing Dictionary*; the memoir *Death Grip: A Climber's Escape from Benzo Madness*, about his escape from benzodiazepine addiction and psychiatric misdiagnosis and over-medication; *Crag Survival Handbook*; and *Colorado Bouldering 2* (with Phillip Benningfield). His climbing adventures have taken him from the high peaks of Colorado, Wyoming, and the Pacific Northwest to the limestone and granite of western Europe.

If You Go

▶ **Getting There:** Several carriers serve Ibiza from Barcelona and Madrid, including Air Europa (800-238-7672; www.aireuropa.com) and Ryanair (+44 8712460002; www.ryanair.com).
▶ **Best Time to Visit**: Early fall through late spring offers the best conditions and fewer crowds.
▶ **Level of Difficulty**: There are routes at Ibiza to suit climbers of all abilities.
▶ **Guides**: The book that brought Matt to Ibiza—*Ibiza Sport Climbing* (David Munilla and Toni Bonet)—remains the most informative guide. Ibiza Vertical Center (www.ibizavertical.com) offers guided climbs.
▶ **Accommodations**: If you're seeking nightlife, find a room in Sant Antoni. Matt preferred the quieter environs at Santa Eularia. Ibiza Spotlight (www.ibiza-spotlight.com) highlights lodging options across the island.

MALLORCA

RECOMMENDED BY **Michael Call**

It's safe to say that Michael Call's first visit to Mallorca made a favorable impression. "The first time I heard about Mallorca was in the early 1990s, from Doug Heinrich, who was a mentor of mine," Mike recalled. "He said that it was one of his favorite places to go for sport climbing. This was before Deep Water Soloing [DWS] was much of a thing. I didn't make it there until 2006, to shoot the movie *King Lines* for Big UP Productions, with the climber Chris Sharma. Filming Chris doing the arch Es Pontas, I was blown away—it was one of the most incredible athletic feats I'd ever seen anyone do.

OPPOSITE:
The Catalan term for Deep Water Soloing is psicobloc, which translates to "psycho-bouldering."

"The day after Chris first climbed Es Pontas happened to be the Feast of San Miguel, and it was also my birthday. We were planning to go back out to Es Pontas, but Chris's fingertips hurt. He suggested that we go to Cova de Diablo. We picked up a bottle of San Miguel beer. When we got to the edge of the cliff, the sun was beginning to go down. Chris suggested I climb with him. We weren't sure who should go first; initially we thought I'd be safer if I went first so he could dive in after me if I fell, but then we decided that if he went first I could follow his line . . . and he could still come in after me. We climbed down a 5.9, then went up a 5.12c, which was pretty tricky for me on sight. But I got through it. Suddenly, we were sitting in a cave about two-thirds of the way up. The sun was setting and there were waves crashing down below. Sitting there, a feeling washed over me—this was why I had learned to rock climb. All the skills I'd gained over my climbing career, all the experiences I'd had, had led to this moment, to allow me to be in this place at this time. That's what Mallorca is to me—why I was meant to learn to rock climb."

Mallorca (or Majorca) is situated some 120 miles southeast of Barcelona and is the largest of the four Balearic Islands. There's a strong sense of identity here; people see themselves as Mallorcan first, Spanish second. Though many people know Mallorca for its beaches, there's a thriving agricultural area in the center of the island—wonderful fresh fruit and vegetables, as well as lamb and goat. Mallorca is especially well known for its almonds, figs, and olives.

And for its Deep Water Soloing opportunities.

To the vertically challenged, many rock climbing endeavors seem to verge on the edge of sanity. It's no wonder, then, that DWS strikes even some in the climbing community as simply crazy. (As Zofia Reych has pointed out on "Up That Rock," the Catalan term for DWS is *psicobloc*, which translates to "psycho-bouldering." The term *fliñar* is also used to describe the activity, which translates roughly as "to crap yourself while at a height." Enough said.) A Mallorcan climber named Miquel Riera is considered the father of DWS, though in a 2016 interview with *Climbing*, he demurred: "Psicobloc has been practiced since the first time there was a climber, a sea cliff, and it was hot. But it wasn't until we began to establish routes, name them, and grade them in Mallorca in 1978 that anyone considered it a sport." With the release of *King Lines* in 2007—the bestselling climbing film of all time (until *Free Solo* in 2018)—Mallorca would be forever associated with psicobloc. In the movie, Chris Sharma had this to say about his amazing feat: "What makes this climb so difficult is that you're upside down, you're hanging on your arms and fingertips the whole time. And on top of that, the wall is absolutely blank for seven feet. You have to actually just kind of leap through the air and stick another hold." It took Sharma nearly one hundred tries to ascend the arch.

To say that Es Pontas is not for everyone is an understatement; in fact, as of this writing, only one other climber, Slovenian Jernej Kruder, has conquered the arch. But the good news is that for the aspiring DWSer, there are also less challenging—and far less daunting—climbs available. "The holds are comfortable and the routes are creative," Mike continued. "In September and October—the prime season for climbing, as the rocks are drier—the water is bathtub warm. It seems perfectly designed for climbers. Many of the cliffs have routes that are only twenty or thirty feet above the water, though most are forty to fifty feet high. Any higher and you'd be horrified! At a place like Cala Barques on Mallorca's east coast, there are some really low routes, and higher, more difficult routes nearby that you can progress to. [Many of the best DWS spots are on the east side of the island.] The lower cliffs are just as beautiful and dramatic, just not as high up. That being said, you don't want to go to Mallorca to DWS as a beginner—even some of the world-class climbers who have visited don't take to the idea of climbing above the water, and people have drowned doing this. [Buoyancy vests are becoming more popular.] But if you have good skills, common sense, and some fellow climbers to help you if you go into the water, it's an unforgettable experience."

Not to mention that there's some first-rate sport climbing on the limestone walls of the island's interior . . . and world-class paella at the end of the day.

MICHAEL CALL got his start shooting rock climbing films in 1988, when he picked up his dad's Handycam and filmed what was going on around him. Since that humble beginning, he's shot, produced, and directed dozens of films and hundreds of shorts, from commercials to feature films, broadcast TV to music videos. Michael's film work includes *Point Break, 127 Hours, Running from Crazy*, and *From the Ground Up*. His television and commercial clients include the National Geographic Channel, NBC, ABC, CBS, BBC, Apple, Ralph Lauren Polo, Adidas, The North Face, and Black Diamond. Michael is based in Salt Lake City.

If You Go

▶ **Getting There:** A number of airlines serve Palma de Mallorca from European cities, including Air Europa (800-238-7672; www.aireuropa.com) and Ryanair (+44 8712460002; www.ryanair.com).

▶ **Best Time to Visit**: Later September and October offer the best rock conditions for aggressive climbers. Those seeking more modest ascents will enjoy the summer months.

▶ **Level of Difficulty**: Psicobloc aspirants should definitely be more seasoned climbers. Mallorca's interior crags offers sport climbing for a wide variety of skill levels.

▶ **Guides:** Several guides will help you explore Mallorca's DSW and sport climbing opportunities, including *Spain: Mallorca* (Alan James, Mark Glaister, and Daimon Beail) and *Psicobloc Mallorca* (Miquel Riera). Rock and Ride Mallorca (www.rockandride-mallorca .com) offers psicobloc instruction.

▶ **Accommodations**: Portocristo rests near the middle of the eastern coastline. Consell de Mallorca (www.infomallorca.net) lists a variety of lodging options.

RÄTIKON

RECOMMENDED BY **Nina Caprez**

Since British mountaineer Edward Whymper first summited the Matterhorn in 1865, climbers of all stripes have been drawn to Switzerland. The Alps stretch across the center of the country, comprising 40 percent of its landmass. Switzerland boasts 437 peaks that eclipse three thousand meters. Although many may equate Switzerland with mountaineering and skiing, the country also boasts a tremendous variety of rock climbing opportunities. Among these, the most celebrated may very well be Rätikon . . . which just so happens to be Nina Caprez's home stomping grounds.

"I grew up near Rätikon," Nina began. "It's a very idyllic place, with many mountains, lakes, valleys with green grass, cows, farmers making cheese—a typical Swiss landscape. The people who live there are very in touch with nature and take good care of it. I was introduced to the mountains at an early age. By thirteen, I followed my older siblings and joined the local climbing club. There were year-round activities—ski-touring in the winter, rock climbing or camping in the spring, alpine climbing on four-thousand-meter peaks in the summer. It gave me an overview of what the mountains had to offer. I always liked rock climbing the most. When you're climbing, you're living fully in the moment. You're confronting yourself, overcoming your fears. Those limestone walls at Rätikon have great meaning, great power. The climbing is very demanding—slabby, vertical, some overhang from time to time. You need solid technique and to trust your feet. If you're mentally centered and healthy, you'll climb well and have a good day. If not, you'll be better off going for a swim in the lake. Climbing at Rätikon is facing the truth."

The Rätikon range rests in the Central Eastern Alps, in the Swiss canton of the Grisons (or Graubünden) near the border with Liechtenstein and Austria. While the range extends some distance and includes a number of peaks over 2,500 meters, for rock

OPPOSITE:
Joe Kinder
prepares to
rappel off
Silbergeier, one
of Rätikon's
signature
routes—and
one of its most
difficult, at 5.14a.

DESTINATION

39

175

climbing purposes, Rätikon references a nine-mile south-facing section of wall between the villages of Schuders (to the west) and St. Antönien (to the east). Given the Swiss proclivity for alpinism, it's not surprising that the Rätikon's climbing history dates back to the early 1600s, when the range's highest peak—Schesaplana (2,965 meters)—was scaled. (All of its peaks were conquered by 1870.) Trad climbing came to the Rätikon in the 1920s and '30s; one of its classic ascents, Schwarzpfeiler on Grosser Drusenturm, was established by Max Niedermann and W. Fleischmann in 1954.

If there are two names (in addition to Nina's) that are associated with the Rätikon in more recent years, they would be Swiss climber Martin Scheel and Austrian Beat Kammerlander. In 1984, Scheel established Amarcord (5.12c) on Kirchlispitzen, one of the early sport climbing milestones in the region. Beat Kaamerlander appeared on the scene in 1989. He started with New Age, which was among the first climbs graded 5.13b. Soon he pushed on to Die Unendliche Geschichte (5.14a), and between 1993 and 1994, he put up and redpointed the infamous Silbergeier (5.14a). Of the many formidable routes at Rätikon, the nearly eight-hundred-foot Silbergeier may be the ultimate test piece. *Planet Mountain* has described it this way: "The route is perfectly vertical and offers super-technical face climbing on small edges and microscopic footholds . . . excellent finger strength is required more than pure muscle strength and, above all, excellent footwork to get to grips with this type of climbing." Though in his late fifties as of this writing, Kaamerlander has not been resting on his laurels. At age fifty-five, he put up Drei Siebe (just over the border in Austria); at fifty-eight, he put up Kampfzone (5.14b).

Nina Caprez has built her fine reputation in part on her completion of challenging ascents on the vertiginous Rätikon massif. These include the third-ever ascent of Headless Children (5.13d), an 850-foot monster; the third climb of 1,377-foot Die Unendliche Geschichte (5.14a), with climbing partner Barbara Zangerl, which had initially been established by Kammerlander; Hannibals Alptraum (5.12d) with Marc Le Menestrel, a test piece first climbed by Martin Scheel and Robert Bösch; and the first female ascent of Silbergeier. When asked about other climbs she enjoys in the region, Infitada (5.12a/b) came to mind. "It's a pretty steep route, even by Rätikon standards," she said, "and very slabby. It's ten or eleven pitches and very pretty."

If you need a break from scaling Rätikon's walls, you might opt to take in their heights from a trail. "There are a number of multiple-day hikes you can do, from hut to hut," Nina added. "Some will take you into Austria and Liechtenstein and back into Switzerland.

[The huts generally provide meals as well as bedding.] If you're looking for a more restful day, you can visit one of the area's cheese production facilities to taste real Swiss cheese."

NINA CAPREZ is a professional sport climber, trad climber, and caver. A native of Switzerland, she's now based in Grenoble, France. Her notable ascents to date (beyond those mentioned above) include Bout'Chou (5.14a), Buoux; Humildes pa casa (5.14a), Oliana; Little Kings (5.14b), St. Ange; Tête de Gondole (5.14a), Boffy; Les braves gens (5.13d), Verdon; Aiztol (5.14b), Margalef; Orbayu (5.14b), Picos de Europa; Carnet d'adresse (5.14a), Grenoble; Dame Cookie (5.13c), Verdon; Délicatessen (5.13d), Corsika; Ali Baba (5.13c), Aiglun; Hotel Supramonte (5.13d), Sardinia; and La Ramirole (5.13d), Verdon. Her sponsors include Petzl, ARC'TERYX, MSR, Scarpa, Prattigau Tourism, Albeina Sport, LYO Food, and Hard Bar. You can follow Nina's adventures at www.ninacaprez.ch.

If You Go

▶ **Getting There:** International travelers will generally fly into Zurich, which is served by many carriers. From there, it's roughly 1.5 hours' drive to Schuders.

▶ **Best Times to Visit**: Spring and fall provide the best climbing conditions.

▶ **Level of Difficulty**: Although there are some less technically challenging climbs here, Rätikon will be most enjoyed by more advanced climbers.

▶ **Guides**: Several guidebooks have been written, but all are in German. A climbing store, Norbert Joos Bergsport (www.bergsport.ch), has a good equipment selection and can provide some intel.

▶ **Accommodations**: Near Schuders, Kletterclub Rätikon operates a hut, Parduzhütte (www.kcr-online.ch). In St. Antönien, two lodging options are Bergrestaurant Sulfluh (+41 813321213; www.kcr-online.ch) and Bergrestaurant Aplenrösli (+41 0813321218). (While camping is officially forbidden, those who leave a light footprint will likely be tolerated.)

DESTINATION

39

HUECO TANKS STATE PARK

RECOMMENDED BY **Stephen Marek**

When asked what makes Hueco Tanks a special place, Stephen Marek had a ready response.

"Not only does Hueco have world-class bouldering, it also has a lot of history. There are now around 3,500 bouldering problems throughout the 860-acre park, and new climbs are still getting put up! The rock is syenite porphyry, an igneous rock that is similar to granite but without all of the quartz. A good chunk of the rock is covered in ironrock, a desert patina formed from clay, iron, and other minerals deposited onto the rock by wind and rain. This patina is what helps protect Hueco's rock from further erosion, and it also provides excellent climbing holds. The problems have varying types of holds and moves, ranging from Hueco jug hauls to thin crimpy faces to even some slopers and slabs. Hueco is a land full of heel hooks and kneebars, so practice before you come! Problems range from V0 up to V15, although many of the 'easier' climbs will seem a bit sandbagged, as a V0 is supposed to be equivalent to about a 5.9 rope climb. You can run into people from all over the world, including pro climbers as they work their new projects.

"We first visited Hueco Tanks in May 2010. It was hot and we barely sent anything, but we were hooked! We left that trip knowing that we would be back for good someday. For the next few years, we spent many weekends and all of our vacation time at the Tanks, eventually moving here in 2016, fulfilling our prediction. There is something very special about Hueco Tanks. An inexplicable, almost spiritual feeling washes over you when you arrive. The climbing is, of course, fantastic, and the scenery is beautiful, but I believe it is this feeling that keeps people coming back time and time again."

Hueco Tanks State Park rests in the Chihuahuan Desert, roughly thirty miles northeast of the city of El Paso. It takes its name from the hollows—*huecos* in Spanish—that

OPPOSITE:
Paul Nelson
puts a move on
Babyface, a V7
in the North
Mountain section
of Hueco Tanks.

DESTINATION

40

179

dot many of the boulders and other rocks in the region. These huecos gather water during the brief rainy season (the area averages eight inches of precipitation a year), providing sustenance for a host of animals. "Though you're in the desert, there are places where you wouldn't realize it," Stephen continued. "Prickly pear cacti, ocotillo, claret cup cacti, sotol, yucca, creosote bushes, and mesquite litter the landscape. However, you can easily find yourself in a small forest of juniper, scrub oak, or other trees. You can't forget that the environment is extremely fragile; simply stepping on a plant may kill it. People have been attracted to this area for nearly ten thousand years, and many of them have left behind traces of their respective cultures. Native American pictographs can be found all over the park, along with pottery shards and arrowheads."

Climbers began exploring Hueco Tanks in 1980, led by John Sherman, Bob Murray, Mike and Dave Head, and Todd Skinner, among others. Within a decade, others began trekking to the Chihuahan for Hueco's seeming endless assortment of problems. It was around this time that Sherman began developing the V-grade scale (derived from his nickname, Vermin) that's become a standard for grading bouldering problems; he also penned the region's first guidebooks. Today, the bouldering is split between four areas— North Mountain, East Mountain, East Spur, and West Mountain. North Mountain grants access for up to seventy climbers a day, with most spots available on a reservation basis; the other sections require that climbers be accompanied by a guide. "The rules for access can seem a bit overwhelming at first, but once you learn them, you'll realize how much they protect the park, our access, and our climbs," Stephen explained. "Keeping the crowds down can be nice; you won't have thirty climbers all under one climb.

"Of the four areas, West Mountain is by far the most rugged and distinct. Many of the approaches are more like scrambles, and they can be scary, especially for first-timers. The climbing areas also tend to be a bit more spread out. However, West is packed with steep roof climbing ranging from V0 to V12+. There are also some steep crimp lines, and an amazing area called the Round Room that has a 150-plus-foot traverse around a room full of huecos. The other mountains are all relatively similar to each other, with a good range of climbing styles: roofs, crimps, jug hauls, and even a few slopers. Grades range from V0 to V15, and there are classics of every grade on every mountain. Typical approaches tend to be easier than West's, and climbing areas tend to be closer together." During the high season, competition for the ten unreserved slots for North Mountain can be intense; sometimes there will be a line of twenty-plus cars at the gate to the park before it opens.

Should you tire of camping fare during your stay at Hueco Tanks, some fine Tex-Mex food awaits you in this border country. "There are a few good options within a fifteen-minute drive from the park," Stephen advised. "Dona Lupitas Tamales is fantastic, but a lot of the climbers go to El Duranguito for burritos. The Vista supermarket also has some pretty tasty burritos that you can buy by the pound. If you're willing to wander farther into town, Julios has great margaritas and Clasico has a huge selection of *micheladas* [a Mexican beer cocktail]."

STEPHEN MAREK is a professional photographer specializing in sports. He was a lecturer at the University of Texas at Austin until 2016. Steve enjoys both bouldering and sport climbing, and operates Blue Lizard Climbing and Yoga (www.bluelizardclimbing andyoga.com) with his wife, Beth.

If You Go

▶ **Getting There:** Hueco Tanks is roughly forty minutes east of El Paso, which is served by a number of carriers.
▶ **Best Time to Visit**: November through March provides the best conditions—though the season can extend a month in either direction if the weather is willing.
▶ **Level of Difficulty**: With more than 3,500 problems, there's something for everyone.
▶ **Guides**: North Mountain can be bouldered on your own, though you'll need advance reservations (available by calling 512-389-891). Climbing the other areas requires joining a tour (contact the park at 915-857-1135) or a commercial guide. Guide services include Blue Lizard Climbing and Yoga (512-843-0963; www.bluelizardclimbingandyoga.com) and Wagon Wheel Coopt (www.wagonwheelcoopt.com). Guidebooks include *Hueco Tanks Climbing and Bouldering Guide* (John Sherman) and *Hueco Tanks* (Matt Wilder), though the latter is out of print.
▶ **Accommodations**: There is limited camping at Hueco Tanks State Park (512-389-8911). Just outside the park, you can find camping, bunk rooms, and private rooms at Hueco Rock Ranch (915-996-3613; www.americanalpineclub.org/hueco-rock-ranch) . . . and many motel options closer to El Paso.

DESTINATION

40

RAILAY BEACH

RECOMMENDED BY **Tar Dindang**

If the idea of climbing giant karst limestone pillars that tower above powdery white beaches and warm turquoise waters has any appeal, you may want to start booking your airline tickets to Thailand: Railay Beach, in the province of Krabi, beckons.

"There are so many routes at Railay," Tar Dindang began. "Every wall along the beach has climbing options. It's very easy to access the climbs, and it's a five-minute walk to the beach for a swim or some coffee or lunch, before you climb again. There's a lot to explore—and there are many restaurants on the beach, and bars where you can hang out with other climbers and hear about other places to climb."

Railay Beach is in the province of Krabi, which sits near the southern end of Thailand, on the Andaman Sea. Tourism is a significant economic driver for the region; during holiday weeks in the winter high season, you'd think that tourism is Krabi's *sole* economic engine. The primary draw, of course, is the juxtaposition of pronounced limestone cliffs—some connected to the mainland, some freestanding in the water—with idyllic beaches and bathtub-warm bays. The limestone karst formations along the Phra Nang Peninsula have an interesting provenance. Hundreds of millions of years ago, they were massive coral reefs. As the ocean waters receded, the coral was slowly broken down by mildly acidic water (thanks to the presence of carbon dioxide in the rain); the resulting cliffs are due more to this chemical process than to erosion, though where oceans meets the karst, erosion does occur. Karst formations are also noteworthy for their extensive cave systems, another geologic feature found around Phra Nang.

The exact genesis of rock climbing in southern Thailand is not completely clear, though it's agreed that the first bolts were put up on the Phi Phi Islands in the late 1980s. (One popular notion of the region's "discovery" is the "James Bond Theory"; the 1974 film *The*

OPPOSITE:

The view from Burnt Offerings. If you enjoy warm turquoise waters, white sand and countless sport climbs, Railay Beach is for you.

DESTINATION

41

183

Man with the Golden Gun featured a karst tower near the island of Ko Tapu in Phang Nga Bay to the north of Pra-Nang, and some believe this may have ignited interest in the area's rock climbing potential.) As observed on the Thaitanium Project website, some Dutch climbers recorded the first ascents at Phi. Soon after, other climbers recognized the potential of the walls, which featured many pockets, stalactites, and stalagmites . . . though the soft rock and lack of natural lines made climbing risky. In 1988, the still relatively new notion of inserting steel expansion bolts was brought to the Phi Phi Islands, and the first local sport climbs were born. In the next few years, the potential of the walls at Railay and Tonsai Bays was discovered, with the first routes going up on 123 Wall and Muay Thai Wall.

It should be noted that while the Dutch expedition were the first *recreational* climbers on the Karst walls of southern Thailand, they were certainly not the first climbers. Thai birds' nest collectors have been scaling the walls of caves to harvest the nests of sea swifts for hundreds of years, as the nests—which are made from male swiftlet saliva—are prized by Chinese gourmets for their nutritional value. (Most are used in bird's nest soup; Hong Kong consumes some one hundred tons of birds' nests each year.) Collectors use a combination of ropes, trellises, and scaffolding to reach the nests, which are only harvested after the young birds have left. Recreational climbers should be extremely careful to avoid any caves or walls where harvesters are at work, as these areas are protected.

There are routes for climbers of every ability at Railay. Given the many vacationers who visit and the proximity of the walls, it's no surprise that many novice climbers make their first ascent here. "If you're a beginner and have never climbed, I would probably take you to the 123 Wall," Tar continued. "There are many beginner routes here, less than thirty meters high, and the location is beautiful. For more experienced climbers, I might go to Tonsai Bay to climb Fire Wall, Melting Wall, or the Nest. Or visit Thaiwand Wall at West Railay Beach." Many feel that Thaiwand, which rises over 650 feet above the Andaman Sea, is the region's signature wall. As Sam Lightner Jr., author of a respected book on Thailand climbing, has noted, the rock is special in a number of ways: it's hollow, so nonclimbers can ascend fixed ropes and ladders all the way through it from behind and emerge thirty meters above the beach; the view from its middle and upper reaches is simply sublime; there are routes for everybody, from "rock-faller-offers" and intermediate crag-hangers through to "rock gymnasts." The rock here is just gorgeous; according to Tar, it looks as if "a nonexistent volcano had poured multicolored lava all down it, leaving tiny and sometimes agonizingly sparse holds along the way."

The warm, moist climate of southern Thailand, combined with minerals in the limestone, has accelerated fatigue on the early bolts placed around the region. A nonprofit organization called Thaitanium Project has been working to install titanium climbing bolts in the south and beyond to create safer climbing conditions.

You'll want to be well fortified to tackle Railay's many sport climbs. A host of Thai staples await you. "For breakfast, we often eat rice and curry," Tar said. "Lunchtime might be pad thai with sliced papaya, or fried chicken with garlic and rice. In the evening, there's tom yum soup, chicken with coconut soup, or massaman, green, or red curry which can be prepared with chicken, beef, or shrimp." You can wash it all down with Chang or Leo Beer.

TAR DINDANG is a co-owner and lead guide at Krabi Rock Climbing. He's been climbing since 2004 and has introduced thousands of people to the sport.

If You Go

▶ **Getting There:** Visitors can fly into Krabi via Bangkok on several carriers, including Thai Airways (www.thaiairways.com). To reach Railay Beach, you'll need to take a quick longtail boat ride.

▶ **Best Time to Visit**: December through April provides the best conditions but also sees the largest crowds.

▶ **Level of Difficulty**: There's something for almost everyone around Railay and neighboring Tonsai Bay.

▶ **Guides**: Several guidebooks are available, including *King Climbers: Thailand Route Guidebook* (Somporn Suebhait) and *Thailand: A Climbing Guide* (Sam Lightner Jr.). Many climbing schools and guides operate around Railay, including Krabi Rock Climbing (+66 950283143; www.krabirockclimbing.com).

▶ **Accommodations**: There are many options around Railay, ranging from backpacker huts to elegant lodges. Your Krabi (www.yourkrabi.com) provides a good overview.

DESTINATION

41

MAPLE CANYON

RECOMMENDED BY **Chuck Odette**

Not everyone can keep climbing into their sixties. Fewer still can conquer new climbing challenges at that age. Chuck Odette, however, is one of those climbers. And he finds that as he enters a new phase of climbing, the overhanging rocks of Maple Canyon are especially beguiling.

OPPOSITE:
Tom Richardson
takes on Loser,
a 5.13a, in the
Cobble Roof wall
of Maple Canyon.

"Maple Canyon lends itself to a style of climbing that I can do at age sixty-three, and still do at an elite level," Chuck began. "My fingers aren't as strong, and I've lost some muscle mass, so can't climb as powerfully as I once did. But I'm still good at hanging on for a long time, and have good overhanging climbing technique. And my knees and core are still strong. Maple Canyon allows for full body climbing; my fingers aren't isolated. You have to do many moves, which makes it gymnastic. All of my climbing experience can be put to good use here. This aspect of Maple Canyon makes it attractive to older climbers."

Maple Canyon is an oasis in the arid landscape that characterizes much of central and southern Utah. Roughly two hours south of Salt Lake City, the tree-bedecked canyon—maples and scrub oak giving way to spruce and Douglas firs as you climb up—is largely situated within the Manti–La Sal National Forest. The canyon is marked by a preponderance of conglomerate—sedimentary rock that's embedded with rounded cobbles that range in size from pebbles to basketballs. Many of the sport climbs here are available right off the dirt road that bifurcates the canyon. Overall, there are some seven hundred bolted routes, ranging from beginner-friendly 5.0s to stomach-churning 5.14s. "It's a beautiful setting, light-colored tan cobblestone, granite, quartzite, and basalt," Chuck described. "In the fall when the leaves start changing colors, the contrasts between the greens, reds, and oranges, along with a little snow at the top of the surrounding peaks, are amazing. There are various

DESTINATION

42

drainages that have come down through the mountains to form the canyon," Chuck continued. "It's kind of like the Red River Gorge [in Kentucky] in that respect. I like that the climbing is generally on fairly large holds, even on the harder routes. You can get on difficult routes—even routes above your ability—and do a large portion of them. That's always gratifying." (Fall is considered the best time to climb Maple Canyon, though given the many north-facing overhangs, it can be cool enough to climb in the summer, and overhangs provide some protection from the rain in the spring.)

Chuck discovered Maple Canyon after an injury temporarily took his local haunt out of play. "I knew some guys who were developing some of the routes at Maple in the late '90s," he recalled. "There were some questions about whether the rock would be durable enough and if expansion bolts would work. The rock did hold up. I put visiting on the backburner, as I was focusing on Logan Canyon near my home. Then I tore a biceps connection to my forearm. I had to take two months off, though I was in really good shape otherwise. I rehabbed and trained, but didn't think I'd climb again at the level I wanted. Around 2000, I made a trip down to Maple. Not too much was developed yet, but I knew it would be good. As I recovered, I began climbing there more often and fell in love with it. I never imagined I would still be climbing at sixty, though this past year [2018], I did one of my hardest routes."

When visiting Maple Canyon, Chuck predominantly finds himself in the vicinity of Pipe Dream, a large cave that sits at the top of the canyon's Right Hand Fork. "Just about every route in Pipe Dream is amazing," Chuck said. "Most are 100 to 120 feet long; some are horizontal, some upside down. For part of my warm-up process, I like a 5.12a called Dry Times. There's a lot of movement, which makes it fun for a route of that grade. La Confienza, a 5.13a, is another part of my warm-up for harder stuff. It's very popular for those looking to tackle their first 5.13a. I've heard many people who get on it say, 'Oh, it's not a 13a—but two months later they're still trying to complete it! Don't Mess with Texas is one of the best 5.13c's I've ever been on. There's a 5.14a called Millennium. I first did it when I was fifty-one; it was an age record at the time. I did it again this year, with an extension called Eulogy." As noted in *Rock and Ice* magazine, Odette "barely stuck the lower V7/8 crux of Millennium and continued onward to a higher V6 crux move, again just barely holding on, two-thirds up the Pipe Dream wall. Odette kept fighting until he managed 'the famous Pipe Dream inverted double knee-bar rest,' where he fried his core but gave his upper body a much-needed reprieve before the final moves. After a lengthy ten minute pause, Odette continued on and 'somehow stuck the final dynamic crux . . . barely . . . two bolts from the top.'"

"You see large groups come up to Pipe Dream, as there are lots of options there," Chuck added. "Many people come up to watch and be inspired, to see what climbing a 5.13+ is all about."

One of Chuck's fondest memories concerns his youngest daughter and a different sort of climbing. "It was around 2001, and my daughter came along with me for the summer as I was doing a year-long road trip," he recalled. "We spent a month and a half in Maple, and she was climbing hard routes for an eleven-year old. She'd climb for a while, then do art stuff. On one occasion, I was climbing and she found a willowy maple nearby. She figured that if she climbed to the top and shimmied out on a limb, she'd have just enough weight to bend the limb and jump to the ground. She was twenty-five feet off the ground and the limb bent until she was only four or five feet off the ground. People were freaking out about the little girl and her dad who wasn't paying attention. I was saying, 'If she gets hurt, she won't do it again.' She didn't. And she did it a few more times.

"I guess this shows that Maple Canyon is a great place for climbers of all ages."

CHUCK ODETTE began climbing in the Tetons in 1979 and has never looked back. An accomplished mountaineer, he turned his interest to sport climbing in the early '90s and has gone on to climb more than one thousand lines at or above 5.12, including more than 240 5.13s and nine 5.14s. Some of his most memorable sport climbs include Beyond the Box (5.14a/b), Logan Canyon, Utah; Afterlife (5.14a/b), near Twin Falls, Idaho; Millennium (5.14a), Maple Canyon, Utah; Freak Out (5.14a), Logan Canyon; and Mexican Rodeo (5.13d), Maple Canyon. Since retiring as Petzl's event and athlete-sponsorship coordinator in 2015, Chuck and his wife, Maggie, have traveled America in their thirteen-foot Scamp trailer home, climbing along the way. He is sponsored by Petzl, Five Ten, and Goal Zero.

If You Go

▶ **Getting There:** Maple Canyon is roughly two hours south of Salt Lake City, which is served by most major carriers.

► **Best Time to Visit**: Fall is prime time to visit, though ample shade (from overhangs) on many routes makes summers bearable and provides respite from spring rains.

► **Level of Difficulty**: Maple Canyon offers sport climbs appropriate for a range of climbing skills.

► **Guides**: Several outfitters offer guided climbs at Maple Canyon, including Red River Adventures (877-259-4046; www.redriveradventures.com).

► **Accommodations**: There is limited improved camping in the canyon, and dispersed primitive camping in the adjacent national forest. There are several lodging options in the nearby towns of Ephraim, Mount Pleasant, and Springdale.

MOAB

RECOMMENDED BY **Noah Bigwood**

The town of Moab sits between Arches and Canyonlands National Parks in southeastern Utah, among a remarkable patchwork of canyons, mesas, and deep river gorges. It's easy to enjoy the thousands of square miles of red rock vistas from the seat of your car . . . though the views are even better from the face of a sandstone wall or tower.

"I started visiting the Moab area in the 1970s with my family, and instantly bonded with the place," Noah Bigwood began. "By college, I was spending weeks and weeks on end, dirtbagging out in the desert. After college, I got a job as a mountain-bike guide in the area to support my climbing lifestyle. I ticked off classics, did route development, and explored more off-piste climbs. Despite all my time exploring, I feel like I've barely scratched the surface. It's never ceased to amaze me how big this desert is. In 2001, I opened a climbing guide service (Moab Desert Adventures). My goal was to give people a taste of the vertical life; it's so easy to be trapped in a horizontal existence. Getting intimate with the cliffs and canyons—things you can only access with a rope—is very moving.

"The Moab region is unique for climbers; there are things here that you can't get anywhere else. The first is the Indian Creek area. What first drew people here were the splitters. Any other crag I've been to will have a handful, but at Indian Creek, there are thousands— thin, medium, fat, really fat. And there are hundreds of miles of climbable cliffs to explore, all relatively simple to access. There's been some development on maybe 15 to 20 percent of the rock, but the opportunities are vast. The first phase of climbing here was seeking out the most obvious lines, the perfect finger cracks and hand cracks. Then came less obvious routes, sometimes connecting intermittent cracks with face climbing. The first famous climb was Super Crack, a splitter to end all splitters. Just plug your hands and feet in and repeat. If you can get to the top, you know hand-jam climbing. Even people who are

advanced in their climbing techniques need time to acclimate at Indian Creek. I took a champion competitive climber there a few years back. He struggled to get up the most remedial routes. It was beautiful in a way to see him stumped at first; but then he figured it out. Many climbers approach routes with their hands first; for them, it's about pulling themselves up. At Indian Creek, your hands are there to hold you in while your legs push you up.

"A big part of the experience of climbing at Indian Creek is camping down at Indian Creek. The first climber's campground was directly under the Super Crack Buttress, in a grove of cottonwoods by a creek. It was utterly magical. But as the area gained popularity there was too much pressure, and it was closed. But the BLM [Bureau of Land Management]—working with Friends of Indian Creek—has established new camp-grounds. Staying there connects you so intimately to the place. There's a lot of camarade-rie. Sitting around the fire, hands throbbing, talking about what you did, what you're excited to do, inspired by the play of light in the clouds, the contrast of the blue sky and red rock—it's a quintessential part of climbing at Indian Creek.

"Tower climbing is also a part of the Moab experience, scaling these iconic chunks of rock that are the last remnants of massive buttes, eroded over eons. Many of the tower climbs around Moab are multi-pitch, generally three to four hundred feet. It might take you one to two hours to get to the base of the towers, then you have a three- or four-pitch climb. Most tower climbs are whole-day affairs. You get up early, hike hard, get sweaty. Then you have to overcome the anxiety of your first pitch, though you've already got one thousand feet of vertical relief under your butt when you make the first move. When you get to the top, the space can be tiny. Some tops are the size of a trash can lid. Others, the size of a small football field. You feel like you're on an island in the sky. For some, it's an overwhelming and terrifying experience; for others, it's so exhilarating, they want to do another one as soon as they're back on the ground. Moab has hundreds. [Owl Rock, in Canyonlands National Park, is one of the most accessible towers; and Castleton Tower, in Castle Valley, is perhaps the most famous one in the region.]

"Moab is known for its desert, but there are also three mountain ranges in the region, including the La Sal Mountains. Deep in the La Sals is a special place called Mill Creek Canyon. There's a band of sandstone there—we think it was superheated during the uplift of the mountains. As it eroded, it formed a magnificent type of rock for sport climb-ing. We've developed hundreds of new sport climbs there. The desert can be hot as Hades in the summer, but Mill Creek Canyon is at eight thousand feet. You can find relief from the heat in this deep gorge with lush deciduous trees and a noisy creek. It makes Moab a year-round climbing destination." It's also worth noting that there's some excellent bouldering near Moab, both at Indian Creek and just outside town at Big Bend. Within ten minutes of Moab is Potash Road, which offers a large selection of classic desert climbs with afternoon shade and no approach hike necessary.

Given that most routes require long approaches and challenging climbs, however, most climbers will experience long days around Moab. Early in his climbing career, Noah had an outing that gives new meaning to a long day. "We were camped at the Super Crack Buttress, and we wanted to climb Lightning Bolt Crack at North Six Shooter," he recalled. "A friend gave us a ride to the beginning of the hike, about eight miles; it's about two hours to the base of North Six Shooter. Lightning Bolt Crack is a 5.11 tower climb; it was considered difficult at the time. We put in a supreme effort to do the climb—it was the classic tower experience of being terrified and exhilarated at the same time. When you land on the summit, you can see all three districts of Canyonlands National Park, and all three mountain ranges. We got back to the road and began hitchhiking back to camp. It was pretty quiet then, not a lot of traffic. But a car came by within thirty seconds. We got in, and the guy drove about a quarter mile and stopped. 'Sorry, I thought I was heading farther,' he said, and dropped us off. We started walking again. Eight miles later, another car came along and took us the last quarter mile to camp. Our other friends were sitting around the campfire drinking beer.

"You can be sure that we joined them!"

NOAH BIGWOOD took to the mountains and cliffs in 1976 and has pursued climbing passionately ever since. In addition to a variety of international trips and competitions, he founded a successful climbing guide service in Moab, Utah, in 2001. Noah received his bachelor's degree in philosophy from Colorado College in 1991 and worked his way from laborer to general contractor over more than twenty-five years in the construction trades. Noah spent seven years coaching competitive youth climbers and directing real estate and construction activities for Momentum climbing gyms. Today, he is focusing his years of passion and experience on founding a chain of fitness facilities centered around climbing and yoga.

DESTINATION 43

► **Getting There:** Canyonlands Airport in Moab has daily flights from Denver on United (800-864-8331; www.united.com). Salt Lake City is served by most major carriers and is a four-hour drive.

► **Best Time to Visit**: You'll find the best conditions in spring and fall, though summer climbing can be had in Mill Creek Canyon.

► **Level of Difficulty**: Any climber—beginner to expert—will find an abundance of routes, though there is a scarcity of moderate climbs below 5.9.

► **Guides**: There are a number of guidebooks covering the Moab area, including *Desert Rock I–IV* (Eric Bjornstad). A number of outfitters provide guided climbs, including Moab Desert Adventures (804-814-3872; www.moabdesertadventures.com).

► **Accommodations**: The Moab Area Travel Council (www.discovermoab.com) lists lodging options, including BLM campgrounds. Campsites are available on a first-come/first-served basis.

ZION NATIONAL PARK

RECOMMENDED BY **Rachel Ross**

"Zion is kind of the wilderness of the rock climbing world," Rachel Ross began. "The routes aren't as known, and it's not a marketable commodity the way Yosemite is. Everyone has beta on Yosemite, but here, even routes that are not obscure might not have been done for three or six months. The sandstone is always changing, and you have to keep up with those conditions and know what preparations are necessary. That makes it always adventurous. I had been a boulderer in Michigan, where I grew up, and learned to trad climb in Zion. When I mention this to some people, they say, 'You learned to climb in Zion and you're still alive?'"

OPPOSITE:
Climbers make
their way up
Moonlight
Buttress in Zion
National Park.

Zion National Park sits in the southwestern corner of Utah, not far from the borders of Nevada and Arizona. Its 232 square miles comprise some of the most picturesque canyon country in North America. With almost a five-thousand-foot variance between its highest and lowest elevations, Zion is home to a broad range of flora and fauna—conifers and mule deer at altitude, juniper and bighorn sheep in the canyons. Though much of the park is desert, Zion is watered by the Virgin River and its tributaries, water that has sustained human life here for more than ten thousand years. The Virgin has also helped carve the park's Navajo sandstone cliffs, a rock type that's common across much of the Colorado Plateau in southern Utah. In some places, the cliffs soar to two thousand feet.

"When many people think of desert climbing, it's towers that come to mind," Rachel continued. "There are a few towers in Zion, but mostly we have walls. It's like the walls of Yosemite are meeting the environs of Jordan. In this respect, Zion is the stepchild of other Western climbing spots. It's often hard to find other climbers here. In Yosemite, it's sometimes hard to get away from them; here, you're happy to come upon other climbers."

Part of the "wilderness" character of Zion comes from the fact that many of the walls are far from the road. "The approaches definitely keep people away," Rachel explained. "If people are new and visiting for a shorter amount of time, I try to recommend areas that are closer to the road. The Confluence, on the east-facing walls of the main canyon, is a good place to start. It's a twenty- or thirty-minute hike in to reach a wall that looks out on the town of Springdale. There are tons of single-pitch routes here and a few multi-pitch as well. Confluence also has a few sport climbs, which are not common at Zion. Cerberus, which is also on the east-facing walls of the main canyon, has some classic intermediate routes. I really like Squeeze Play [5.10a] and Cynthia's Handjob [5.10]. One downside of Cerberus is that since it's right off the road, shuttle buses will often stop, and the driver will point out climbers on the wall. When they're idling, you can't hear what your partner is saying. On the more advanced side, there are a number challenging routes in the 5.11 class on the Watchman, a mountain in town. Iron Messiah [5.10b], on the Spearhead wall, is another test piece, a ten-pitch route that climbs one thousand feet." If you're itching to climb a tower, Ataxia is a good bet; Ashtar Command [5.9] is a popular route here.

The town of Springdale, which is just east of the park boundary, is a good base of operations. "There are lots of hotels and restaurants," Rachel said, "and there's nearby federal land if you don't want to camp in the park. Parkhouse Café is the go-to breakfast spot. For dinner, there's the Bit and Spur, which has Southwestern food and margaritas. Oscar's Café is another dinner spot. It has the biggest burgers and sweet potato fries."

If you need a break from climbing, Rachel would encourage you to try canyoneering. "On one level, it's the exact opposite of climbing," she explained. "I hated it at first—the idea of rappelling into a place where I might have to swim. But I've come to love it. I think it's more problem-solving-oriented than climbing, and definitely more team-oriented. In climbing, you have to have a decent level of skills to get in trouble; in canyoneering, you don't use your skills until you've dropped down and have to problem-solve. When I'm canyoneering, I feel like I'm interacting more with the environment, understanding how I fit in—can I bolt this rock? How deep is this water? When did it rain last? You see how the desert is constantly evolving."

Rachel had conquered Iron Messiah before. But it was when she tackled the wall with a visiting friend that the magnitude of the accomplishment really resonated. "Taking my friend to Iron Messiah was a culmination of all my skills and all the things I love. First you have the approach, where you have to veer off the main trail into a no-man's-land, scrambling over scree, grabbing on to bushes to hold on—an adventure in itself. When we started climbing, some of the holds I remembered from my previous climb were broken. When we reached the chimney pitches on the climb, we had to squeeze in and use our whole bodies—later you have bruises on your thighs! At the top, you've reached someplace that no one else can get to unless they're climbing.

"For me, this is what rock climbing in Zion is all about."

RACHEL ROSS is a photographer, videographer, and website designer, with an affinity for the desert and a passion for expeditions. She is a canyoneering guide based just outside Zion National Park whose adventures have taken her from Patagonia to Tibet. Rachel is an avid climber, canyoneer, runner, biker, and painter, and has been fortunate enough to combine these passions in different permutations to capture moments of adventure, joy, and creativity. Her clients include *Adventure Pro Magazine*, Goal Zero, Zion Adventure Company, Marriot International, and Dell Computers.

If You Go

▶ **Getting There:** The closest commercial airport is in St. George (an hour's drive from the park), which is served by several carriers, including Delta (800-221-1212; www.delta.com) and United (800-864-8331; www.united.com).

▶ **Best Time to Visit**: Early spring and fall offer the best conditions.

▶ **Level of Difficulty**: There are options to suit climbers of a wide range of abilities, though there's not an abundance of beginner terrain.

▶ **Guides**: Several outfitters guide climbers in Zion, including Zion Adventures (435-772-1001; www.zionadventures.com). *Zion Climbing: Free and Clean* (Bryan Bird) will help point you in the right direction, though be aware that conditions in the park change frequently.

▶ **Accommodations**: Camping is available in the park at Watchman Campground (877-444-6777; visit www.recreation.gov). Other lodging options in Springdale and surrounding towns are highlighted at Zion Canyon Visitors Bureau (www.zionpark.com).

NORTH CASCADES

RECOMMENDED BY **Larry Goldie**

Larry Goldie discovered the North Cascades because he wanted to get out of the rain. "Twenty-five years ago I lived in Bellingham, on the west side of the Cascades on the coast of Washington," he began. "I started making forays to the east side of the mountains. I found that when it was pouring down rain in Bellingham, it would often be warm and sunny on the east side. There was also some very high-quality granite."

With more than two million acres to their name, the North Cascades are perhaps the largest wilderness area in the continental United States that you've never heard of. They extend from Lake Chelan in the south to the border with British Columbia in the north, and encompass a large swath of the Cascade Mountains in between. The nexus of rock climbing in the North Cascades is Washington Pass, on Highway 20, just outside of North Cascades National Park in the Okanogan National Forest. "One of the reasons that the pass is the epicenter is that it's the high point of the road," Larry continued. "You're in the mountains as much here as anywhere on the highway. Another reason is that you have easy access to a huge exposed chunk of granite, the Liberty Bell Massif, which includes Liberty Bell, Concord Tower, Lexington Tower, and North and South Early Winters Spires. They are just a short hike away."

Larry recommended a few trad climbs for Washington Pass newcomers of different abilities. "For folks with little climbing experience, there's South Arête on South Early Winters Spire, the tallest spire here. There's a little bit of technical roped climbing at the bottom; but the rest is mostly scrambling—though it's very exposed at spots. Most climbers will use a rope the whole way, but you don't need a ton of experience to do the climb. One of the classic intermediate climbs is the Beckey Route [5.6] on Liberty Bell, one of many first ascents Fred Beckey had in the North Cascades. He had a knack for

OPPOSITE:
The North Cascades provide a broad range of trad climbs on quality granite, on Washington's sunnier side.

establishing some of the best climbs. There are four pitches, and each requires a wide range of climbing techniques. Another very good intermediate route is Southwest Rib (5.8) on South Early Winters Spire. It's nine pitches—hard enough to feel like you're really climbing, easy enough that most people can do it. There are beautiful belay ledges at the top of each pitch to break up the climbing. A few pitches put you in unique aesthetic positions. One, near the top, puts you right at the crest of an exposed spine. On Beckey and Southwest Rib, you're looking out at the heart of the national park, with big glaciers, Glacier Peak, and Mount Baker in the distance.

"More advanced climbers will want to tackle Liberty Crack [5.11a], a 1,200-foot sheer face on the east side of Liberty Bell—it's what you see from the Washington Pass Overlook. Liberty Crack is a continuous crack system that works its way up the areas' biggest wall. It requires a few pitches of aid climbing early on—it's not difficult if you have some aid climbing experience. The free climbing is outstanding. It's definitely a jump up in difficulty from Beckey and Southwest Rib, but still within the realm of possibility for many climbers. If you don't have aid climbing experience, it's a 1.5-day affair. Hitchhiker [5.11] is another great advanced climb, on the southeast face of South Early Winters Spire. It's sustained, but the rock is high quality. Looking east from either climb, you'll see the craggy massifs of Wine Spires and Silver Mountain. These are also great climbing destinations, but it takes twice as long to approach them."

If you have a yen for a multiday backcountry trip, Larry might point you to West Ridge on Forbidden Peak in the national park. "There's a bit of everything involved," he described. "An arduous approach on a climber's trail over logs and raging streams, a small glacier and snow couloir to navigate, and then a long exposed fourth and low fifth class ridge up to a dinner table–size summit. The climbing isn't too complicated, but it's a difficult descent. For variety and positioning, it's tough to beat."

Post-climbing, many retire to the nearby hamlet of Mazama. "The Mazama Store has an unbelievable bakery and deli," Larry enthused, "and great coffee and beer on tap. In the summer, there's live music. There's also a great gear shop, the Goat's Beard. If you live in a rural place and can only have one store, this is the one you want."

The North Cascade's remoteness—one of its defining features—speaks to one of Larry Goldie's fondest climbing memories. "There are some climbs I do every year," he ventured. "They're so good and so fun. A buddy and I were going to tackle one of those climbs. As we were driving, we passed a spire, one of the smaller peaks in the area. I'd driven by it many times, and I'd recently caught sight of a ridgeline that I didn't think had been climbed. I mentioned to my friend that we should do it some time. My friend said, 'How about right now?' We spun the car around and we climbed it. It was a first ascent. And now it's considered a moderately classic route. We named it Spontaneity Arête. In the North Cascades, there are still unclimbed lines, especially if you don't mind hiking in a bit farther. It gives me comfort that in this day in age, you can still find a chunk of rock that hasn't been climbed."

LARRY GOLDIE, co-owner and lead guide for North Cascades Mountain Guides, has been making a living as a mountain guide for over two decades. He has climbed, skied, and guided extensively in the Cascades, as well as the Alps, Sierras, Rockies, Alaska, and Canada. An International Federation of Mountain Guides Associations licensed mountain guide and an American Mountain Guide Association certified guide, Larry is an instructor for AMGA and an instructor trainer and pro course instructor for American Institute for Avalanche Research and Education.

If You Go

▶ **Getting There:** Mazama is roughly 3.5 hours from Bellingham, which is served by Alaska (800-252-7522; www.alaskaair.com) and Allegiant (702) 505-8888; www.allegiant air.com), and 4.5 hours from Seattle, which is served by many major carriers.

▶ **Best Time to Visit:** July and August are the best times to climb here, though the season can extend a month on either side.

▶ **Level of Difficulty:** There are some routes suited to less experienced climbers, but more of the terrain here is better suited for intermediates and above.

▶ **Guides:** Several companies lead climbing trips in the North Cascades, including North Cascades Mountain Guides (509-996-3194; www.ncmountainguides.com). Fred Beckey's *Cascade Alpine Guides* remain classic resources for climbers.

▶ **Accommodations:** There are several forest service campgrounds in the area, including Klipchuk. Mazama has several lodges (highlighted at www.mazama.org); there are more-modest motels just down the road in Winthrop (www.winthropwashington.com).

DESTINATION

45

NEW RIVER GORGE

RECOMMENDED BY **Paul Nelson**

When Paul Nelson landed a professorship in Ohio, he had a decision to make. "Ohio was a flatter place than I was used to," he recalled. "I soon realized that the city where I was teaching was equidistant between the Red River Gorge and the New River Gorge. I visited both and was drawn to the New. Something about the New hit me—it was reminiscent of the climbing I was used to out west, around Indian Creek, but with better face holds. The rock quality around New River Gorge is tremendous. I'm a sandstone aficionado, and here you have some of the oldest sandstone anywhere, bullet hard. It's weathered, you can get friction, but it's also very solid. You can really trust your feet and your gear. New River has the finest single-pitch cragging I've done anywhere.

"A few years after moving to Ohio, I got the chance to run a campground down at New River, and I moved to Fayetteville, the region's hub town. It's an outdoor tourist town, but with a significant difference—we're in West Virginia. The vibe in some outdoors recreation towns is expensive. That's not the case in Fayetteville. The cost of living is cheap, and the place hasn't been gentrified. It has an old-school Appalachian component. Many of the guides who work the crags and the rivers here are natives."

The New River Gorge is in south-central West Virginia. Once a coal-industry center, the region saw its last mine close in the 1950s. The decline of extractive industries has been extremely hard on the local economy, but the possibilities of ecotourism in the form of rafting, rock climbing, and mountain biking hold some hope. When climbers reference the area as a destination, they are really referencing three distinct areas: the New proper, the Meadow River Gorge, and the Gauley River Gorge/Summersville region. Paul elaborated on their differences: "The New is part of a protected national scenic river area. It's very tightly regulated. There are both trad and sport climbs here, but it's very difficult to put up

OPPOSITE:
Karsten Delap approaches the summit of Two Bag Face on Fern Buttress, one of New River Gorge's most beautiful and fun-to-climb routes.

DESTINATION

(46)

new bolts. The New is the upper-class neighborhood of the region, with gentrified climbs and not much litter. The Meadow, on the other hand, is more blue collar, a rough-and-ready place. There are old railroad grades by the cliffs, and there will often be ATVs and dirt bikes roaring around. It's the Wild West out there, and you can do what you want—camp at the base of the cliffs, bolt whatever you want. Some of the bolting is not well done, but there's great potential for new routes. Then there's Summerville. I think of it as the Disneyland of the area's climbing. It has the highest concentration of moderate bolted routes, as well as harder but fun steep routes. In the summertime the humidity is oppressive, but the lake is right there. You can work on a few projects and then cool off in the water."

Climbers began exploring the New River Gorge in the 1970s, particularly at the Bridge Buttress and Beauty Mountain areas. But it was in the '80s that the sandstone here began attracting more attention. Climbers like Doug Reed, Cal Swoager, and Lynn Hill began putting up harder and harder routes—including Hill's first ascent of the Greatest Show on Earth (5.13a), at Lower Meadow on the Meadow River Gorge. Today, it would be difficult to find any climber—trad or sport—who hasn't at least heard of the New River Gorge.

There are fine climbs to be had across the New River Gorge region—primarily sport at Meadow and Summerville, a fairly even mix at New River proper. Paul is a bit partial to the New River Gorge, which is home to more than 1,400 routes. He ticked off a few favorites: "Endless Wall has miles of routes. There's a lifetime of trad climbs for those who are comfortable at 5.10. Party in My Mind [5.10b] on the Party Buttress is my favorite moderate trad climb, a must-do. Burning Calves [5.10b] on Burning Buttress is a fine climb, as is Springboard [5.10b], an elegant finger crack route, and Quick Robin, to the Batcrack! [5.10a]. Some noteworthy harder trad climbs at New River include Color Blind [5.13a] at Honeymooner's Area; the crux here is very intimate, but protected. The South Nuttall Crag has some amazing 5.12 cracks. The cracks such as the New Traditionalists [5.12b] are like they were laser cut. For sport climbs, Legacy [5.11a] is the best pitch at 5.11—just follow the cracks. The Gift of Grace [5.12b], at Diamond Point, is my favorite 5.12. There's a crag called the Cirque that's got a prominent overhang. It's the last one to get wet. A route there, Skylore Engine [5.13a], is a full-value one-hundred-foot pitch. When 5.13 climbers from Red River Gorge come to climb, they often get shut down on Skylore."

Fayetteville provides an inviting atmosphere for visiting outdoors people—climbers, rafters, and mountain bikers. "For breakfast, you should visit Cathedral Café," Paul described. "It's an institution, situated in an old repurposed church. There's a great pizza place called Pies & Pints. It was started by some river guides in a basement, and now it's grown to be one of the most successful pizza franchises in the mid-Atlantic States. My personal favorite is a farm-to-table restaurant called the Station. It's the local climbers' hangout; it has crushed many climbing careers with its margaritas. After dinner, there's a great music scene. Almost all the local bars have live bands. I'm a jazz guitarist on the side, and I can play three gigs a week if I want."

PAUL NELSON currently lives in Fayetteville, West Virginia, where he is a public school teacher. He has been climbing for twenty years and, in that time, has dabbled in most forms of rock climbing around the United States, Canada, and Mexico, from big walls to bouldering. Paul favors sandstone, cracks, and traditional protection. Indian Creek, the Gunks, and the New River Gorge are his favorite crags. When he's not climbing, he plays bluegrass mandolin and jazz guitar, and writes. He's also a historian and has written a history of Utah's Canyon Country, *Wrecks of Human Ambition*. Paul is sponsored by Misty Mountain Threadworks.

If You Go

▶ **Getting There:** The nearest commercial airport is in Charleston, West Virginia, which is served by a *limited* number of carriers. From here, it's roughly fifty miles to Fayetteville. The nearest major airport is in Pittsburgh, three hours away.

▶ **Best Time to Visit:** The best conditions are found from late March to mid-June and from mid-September to late November.

▶ **Level of Difficulty:** Climbers who are comfortable at 5.10 trad and 5.11 sport will have fun here.

Guides/Outfitters: There are several guidebooks for the region, including the two-volume *New River Rock* (2nd ed., Mike Williams). Several guide services lead climbers in the gorges, including New River Mountain Guides (304-760-9791; www.newriverclimbing.com).

▶ **Accommodations:** There are a number of campgrounds in the region, including the American Alpine Club Campground (https://lodging.americanalpineclub.org). A variety of other lodging options are highlighted at Visit Fayetteville (www.visitfayettevillewv.com).

DESTINATION

46

SENECA ROCKS

RECOMMENDED BY **Arthur Kearns**

A rich climbing history, challenge, relentless exposure—and all within a day's drive of nearly half of America's population. It has to be Seneca Rocks.

"Seneca plays an important role in the history of East Coast climbing," Arthur Kearns explained. "The first recorded ascent was made in 1939 by Paul Brandt, Don Hubbard, and Sam Moore. But when they got to the top, there were initials: "D.B. Sept. 16, 1908." So they obviously weren't the first. I first climbed Seneca in 1988. When I got to the top, I could still make out the initials. Now it's all worn away. [In *Seneca: The Climber's Guide*, Bill Webster attributes the initials to a surveyor name Bittenger.] The 10th Mountain Division used Seneca as a training ground during World War II, in preparation for engagements in Italy. They'd bring in men for two- to three-week periods. The men were vetted—those who showed climbing promise were taught advanced climbing; those who didn't received support training. They drove an unbelievable number of pitons—over seventy-five thousand—up in North Fork Valley. You'll still find World War II pitons in the rocks. The groups trained there went on to be the main assaulters at Riva Ridge.

"Seneca has a mystique about it, a reputation for having visitors come and have their eyes opened. When climbing started in the '30s and '40s, 5.9 was the hardest rating. It was a time when people had a bit more humility. There was a pre-Facebook mentality, and people were climbing for themselves. I think routes were graded on a more humble level. You can get on things today that were rated 5.8 then that might have a solid 5.10 now; there are 5.9s that have turned into 5.10s . . . and some people feel should be 5.11s. Take Solar, which is rated 5.7. It was put up by a guy with hobnail boots and a rack of pins. As one older climber I know says, 'It was a special day when everybody in my group had their own carabiner.' You go up there now, you're glad you have modern equipment. Another

OPPOSITE:
Nicky Dyal is
all smiles on
the summit of
North Peak.

DESTINATION

47

part of the mystique is how vertical and exposed Seneca is. You can climb at any number of places, and the walls wrap around you. By contrast, Seneca is almost all exposed. Even a route like Skyline Traverse, where you have to make a 5.2 move to go across a chasm—you're 150 feet off the ground. It gets in your head pretty quick."

Seneca Rocks and the Spruce Knob–Seneca Rocks National Recreation Area are part of the Monongahela National Forest: 919,000 acres of rugged, mountainous public terrain along the eastern edge of West Virginia. The formation looms some nine hundred feet above the North Fork River, a monolith of Tuscarora sandstone that's long attracted land-bound onlookers as well as climbers. For climbers in the mid-Atlantic region seeking multi-pitch challenges, it's one of the only options around. But what an option! "The rock is bullet hard," Arthur continued. "And most holds are ridiculously solid, even the tiny feet." For climbers visiting the first time, Arthur has some sound advice. "I encourage people to *not* start comparing route classifications with numbers at other places they've climbed. If you do, it's likely to be a bad day. If someone comes by our shop and says they've been climbing a certain grade, we suggest they back off a bit until they get a feeling for the rock. Some are receptive to this advice, others let their ego get in the way . . . and then get their heads handed to them."

For newcomers, Old Man's (5.2) is a great introduction to Seneca. "It's the classic way people go up the first time," Arthur described. "It has three pitches. We use it to teach our intro to alpine climbing, as there are so many rope transitions—multi-pitch to short roping and short pitching. There aren't many places like this on the East Coast. Gunsight to South Peak [5.3] is another classic. You step out on the west face, which gets lots of wind. You're doing exposed moves with the wind blowing, which adds drama and excitement. Once you get accustomed to the conditions, there's an abundance of super-strong moderate routes in the 5.5-to-5.8-class. They're all five star, each unique in its own way. You might climb three 5.7s at another venue and find that you're using the same climbing style. Here, the routes will be quite different, and you'll have a chance to use different techniques. You can do a variety of routes at Seneca, get to the summit, and have a great day. You don't have to put up a difficult grade. And since the fin runs north to south, it's easy to chase the light or shade." When the day is done, many climbers will retire to Harper's Old Country Store. "You can get a pizza upstairs and a six-pack downstairs, then hang out on the picnic tables in front and swap tales," Arthur added.

There's a supportive, friendly environment to be found at Seneca Rocks—perhaps a testament to the humble nature of the area's earliest alpinists. "When you come down after your first ascent—whatever route you take—people revel in your success," Arthur said. "People are stoked, and there's no one-upping. Though when you get to the top, it's a little harrowing. On North Peak you're three hundred feet up, and it's only five feet wide. When my wife Diane first climbed it, she was petrified to stand up."

ARTHUR KEARNS started climbing in 1976. He has been teaching rock climbing since 1988 and views himself as a teacher first and foremost. Climbing has taken Arthur across the United States, including most of North Carolina, the Gunks, North Conway, Joshua Tree, Yosemite, and many more. Internationally, he has climbed in Canada, Bolivia, Greenland, Norway, and France. During the winter, Arthur enjoys telemark skiing the backcountry. In addition to teaching rock climbing, he spends much of his time managing the Gendarme climbing shop (304-567-2600). He is an AMGA Certified Rock Instructor and holds a Wilderness First Responders medical certification.

If You Go

► **Getting There:** The nearest commercial airport is Shenandoah Valley, which is eighty miles away and served by United (800-864-8331; www.united.com). Dulles International is roughly 150 miles distant.

► **Best Time to Visit**: March through November is climbing season, with the best conditions in the fall.

► **Level of Difficulty**: Though there's exposure on every route, Seneca offers a great deal for almost everyone.

► **Guides**: Several guide services lead trips, including Seneca Rocks Climbing School (304-567-2600; www.climbseneca.com). *Seneca: The Climber's Guide*, 2nd ed. (Tony Barnes) is a popular reference.

► **Accommodations**: There are two campgrounds—Seneca Shadows (www.recreation .gov) and Princess Snowbird, part of Yokum's Vacationland (www.yokum.com). (Princess is better for late-night folks.) The town of Seneca Rocks has a number of cabin/motel options.

DESTINATION

47

DEVIL'S LAKE

RECOMMENDED BY **John Wowczuk**

Illinois is the second flattest state in the United States. It's no surprise, then, that an aspiring climber living in the Windy City would be looking elsewhere to find rock.

"When I learned to climb, it was a fringe thing," John Wowczuk began. "Today, there's a climbing gym on every corner, but that wasn't the case when I started. There was nothing close to Chicago where I grew up; but three hours to the north in Wisconsin there was a place called Devil's Lake. I was fortunate to be part of a scouting program, and a few of the leaders in the troop had an interest in climbing. They mentored me. I seemed to have a knack for it—I was doing things in hiking boots that I should've had technical climbing shoes for. I remember those first trips up there. You're driving through rolling hills and typical Midwest farmland. When you reach Wisconsin Lake at the village of Merrimac, you head onto a ferry that takes you across. For a young kid, it was like being spirited off to a faraway land. After crossing the river, you're on winding roads until you come around a corner and these big bluffs appear out of nowhere. The setting can't be beat—especially in the fall, when the leaves are changing."

An hour north of Madison and two hours west of Milwaukee, Devil's Lake State Park is Wisconsin's most popular state park, seeing nearly three million visitors each year. The park includes part of the Baraboo Range, which is made up of Baraboo quartzite—a Precambrian rock formation that dates back as far as 1.5 billion years. Many come to boat, fish, ride bikes, and enjoy the lake's sandy beaches, and an increasing number come to sample those quartzite cliffs.

Though it may lack the notoriety of some locales, Devil's Lake has a long and rich climbing history. Fritz Wiessner, who accomplished many first ascents across North America (including Devils Tower in Wyoming) and nearly tamed K2 in 1939, climbed

OPPOSITE:
A climber takes
on the ubiquitous
purple Baraboo
quartzite on
Brinton's Crack
Direct, Brinton's
Buttress, in
East Rampart,
Devil's Lake
State Park.

213

DESTINATION

48

here in 1942. He was stymied by a line that was then completed by Bill Brinton and is now known as Brinton's Crack (5.6). (Not to be outdone, Wiessner soon went on to establish Wiessner's Face [5.4]). Joe Stettner (of Stettner's Ledges fame) also left his mark here, sending Cleo's Needle (5.4), a lakeside spire in the Cleo's Amphitheater area. Writing in *Climbing*, Jay Knower noted that Cleo's Needle climbers will come upon a bolt on the climb that reads "Joe 1964" (Stettner was a metalworker as well as a talented climber). In 1968, Son of Great Chimney, possibly America's first 5.12, was put up by local physician Pete Cleveland. In the '80s and '90s, Devil's Lake was the home stomping grounds of the Devil's Lake Fukness Association (or DLFA), a collective of climbers known almost as much for their fondness for beer (and, it's rumored, stronger substances) as for their aggressive first ascents. How did one qualify for membership in this group of hard-climbing misfits? Knower quotes fellow climber David Groth this way: "After you burned through all the safe leads, you started doing the not-so-safe ones, and then you got noticed by the DLFA guys."

"The climbing at Devil's Lake is very challenging, and not for the faint of heart," John continued. "The quartzite has this purplish color and isn't found anywhere else. It's really slick. It's all trad climbing there, and there's a very old-school ethic. You have to have some gumption to take the lead. Though there's not too much above 5.10 or 5.11, the ratings can be misleading. I've put 5.13 climbers out on a 5.8 at Devil's Lake, and they've had melt-downs." The more than 1,600 routes at Devil's Lake are mostly spread among four cliffs—the East, West, South, and Sandstone Bluffs. A majority of ascents are on the East and West Bluffs, and most are one hundred feet or less. John provided some guidance for first-time visitors. "I'd send you along to East Rampart on the East Bluff," he said. "It's the most exposed cliff band, and there are hundreds of climbs. You should definitely try Brinton's Crack [on Brinton's Buttress]. It gives you the full experience. Upper Diagonal [5.9] is another climb I really like. It's a very aesthetic route on a left-arching diagonal crack. It's so popular, it took me ten years of visits to finally get on it."

Most who've visited Devil's Lake agree that the community—in good midwestern fashion—is very friendly and welcoming. "It's a very popular spot for groups," John described, "and you'll often see four or five ropes dropped in one area. If you ask a group if you can use one of their ropes, they're usually fine with that. It can be slammed on summer weekends and holidays; a lot of people will come up for the day from the cities." After climbing, some will retire to the North Shore Chateau, which offers libations from a small store and a lakeside deck to soak up the last of the day's sun . . . and a Friday-night fish fry Memorial Day through Labor Day.

With the lake nearby for a cooling swim (and, perhaps, the promise of the Friday fish fry), summers are a pleasant time to enjoy Devil's Lake. Given his druthers, however, John would prefer the fall. "I have many happy memories of climbing with a buddy on a beautiful September or October day, wearing fleece, the sun on my face," he reminisced. "On days like that, you catch yourself smiling as you belay your partner up."

JOHN WOWCZUK is a midwesterner at heart, but the wild mountains of the west drew him away . . . for now. His exposure over the past twenty-plus years to this amazing sport and all its disciplines has to lead him to travel the world and meet many great friends, and ironically he has become more "grounded" by all of these experiences. John currently lives in Salt Lake City with his wife, Stephanie, as they try to find the balance with climbing in life. He currently serves as assistant manager for Petzl's sports division.

If You Go

▶ **Getting There:** Visitors can fly into Madison, Wisconsin; Milwaukee; or Chicago, which are one, two, and three hours' driving distance from Devil's Lake.

▶ **Best Time to Visit:** The climbing season is mid-April to mid-October. Early fall is a favorite time.

▶ **Level of Difficulty:** There are routes for people of nearly all abilities here, though some feel the ratings are easier than the climbs.

▶ **Guides:** Several guidebooks are available, including *Climber's Guide to Devil's Lake* (Sven Olof Swartling) and *Devil's Lake: A Climbing Guide* (Jay Knower). Devil's Lake Climbing Guides (608-616-5076; www.devilslakeclimbingguides.com) leads climbs.

▶ **Accommodations:** Camping is available at Devil's Lake State Park (https://wisconsin .goingtocamp.com/). Other lodging options are available in the town of Baraboo (www .baraboo.com).

DESTINATION

48

DEVILS TOWER

RECOMMENDED BY **Frank Sanders**

For some Native American people, the 1,267-foot monolith rising majestically from the high prairie in northeastern Wyoming represents a gesture by the Great Spirit to rescue children from a giant bear. For moviegoers, it's the destination for a group of extraterrestrials. For climbers, it's one of the finest crack climbing venues in the world.

"When I started climbing, I'd say that my scope was small and my ego was big," Frank Sanders began. "In my head, I'd climbed out the East Coast—or at least I'd sampled it. Jim Morrison sang, 'The west is the best,' and I set my sights there. I asked my mentors where I should go, and they said, 'Devils Tower—you won't have a problem with route-finding, just follow the crack.' In June 1972, I hitchhiked out from Tennessee with a friend, and we climbed to the top . . . repeatedly. It was kind of scary, as there simply weren't any other climbers around. My partner and I returned at the end of the summer, and ended up completing the 999th and 1,000th ascents of the tower in its climbing history, since 1937. That's how far climbing was from the mainstream at the time. I went back out in 1976 after grad school, as I'd landed a job as a seasonal ranger at the monument.

"After all these years it is still a mystery to some why people go way out of their way to visit—today there are almost 400,000 park visitors a year. It *is* a huge rock. However, it's not lit up at night, it doesn't move, there's not a waterfall nearby. There aren't any movie theaters or luxury hotels nearby, like many other parks. All that I can conclude is that folks are called from all over to experience the magic and the power of the Tower."

Of those 400,000 visitors, 1,500 to 2,000 of them summit Devils Tower each year. How times have changed!

Resting at the western edge of the Black Hills, Devils Tower is as amazing in its columnar grandeur as in its juxtaposition with the surrounding Great Plains from

OPPOSITE:

Tiffany Campbell takes on Carol's Crack on Devils Tower, one of the American West's most confounding rock formations.

DESTINATION

49

where it implausibly springs. The Tower has great spiritual significance. To some indigenous peoples—including the Lakota, Cheyenne, Crow, Arapahoe, Shoshone, and Kiowa—the monolith is Bears Lodge. (In the Sioux creation legend, the rock sprung up to save seven girls from a giant bear; the tower's columns are a result of the bear's claw marks as he attempted to reach them. After the bear left, the seven girls were lifted into the sky, where they can be seen today as the seven stars in the constellation Pleiades.)

Devils Tower holds a prominent place on the climber's pantheon of must-visit destinations. "All those cracks make it a multi-pitch trad climber's dream," Frank continued. "There are more than two hundred crack climbs that go anywhere from 5.7 to 5.12. One little quirk to know is that these are really East Coast grades. The East Coast grades are the stiffest; as you work your way west, the grades get softer. The first routes were put up by Fritz Wiessner and Jack Durrance, both East Coast folks, back in the '30s. Take the Durrance Route. A lot of people stroll up to it, figuring it can't be that difficult at 5.6. They get their ass handed to them. There is really no 'easy way' to the tower top. The grade here starts at difficult, then goes to harder, then goes to OMG . . . and then WTF! If you can climb grades here, you can climb them anywhere." Though more difficult routes have emerged since the pioneers first ascended Devils Tower, the routes they established—particularly Durrance—still hold an appeal.

For newcomers to Devils Tower, Frank recommends an early start. "Durrance—and most of the other moderate routes—are on the south side of the tower," he explained. "You want to get out there before it's baking hot, so that you can find your own spot. Even though we're not in the mountains, afternoon thundershowers can come out of nowhere and rain lightning on the Tower. Optionally, if the skies are clear and you have enough daylight, you can climb the Durrance Route, starting after two P.M., as that corner of the south side comes into shade at that time. Finding yourself approaching sunset, at the top with a sandwich in one hand and a Gatorade in the other, is a special feeling. You can watch the sun go down behind Little Missouri Buttes, watch the moon rise, and see the stars come out. Then, when the time is right, you switch on your headlamps and rappel down, through the dark. The headlamp shows you everything you need to see; if you rappel after sunset, you avoid looking down seven hundred feet when you step off the top. You only see as far as your headlamp shines. It's like Mother Night wraps her arms around you and says, 'It's OK, you don't have to look.'"

Frank Sanders can tell tales of violent storms engulfing the tower, of harrowing new lines. But his fondest memories of Devils Tower concern visitors finding that they were stronger or more clever then they thought they were. "It's about problem solving," he ventured, "and what a wonderful, dramatic context to overcome problems. The height may seem oppressive. But once you engage it, it's an uplifting experience. If you wrestle with the rock, you're likely to lose. But if you look at the rock with a lover's eyes, the stone will show you right where to touch and how hard to touch."

FRANK SANDERS is one of the greatest resources on Devils Tower culture, history, and climbing. He has topped the tower more than two thousand times and has helped hundreds of climbers make their ascent. Frank owns and operates Devils Tower Lodge, a comfortable bed-and-breakfast in the shadow of the tower, and still leads climbers up his favorite routes. Life has been good to Frank. His climbing adventures have taken him all over this country, Canada, and Mexico. In addition to climbing, Frank enjoys playing piano, sea kayaking, and sewing quilts.

If You Go

▶ **Getting There:** It's a hundred-mile drive to the Tower from Rapid City, South Dakota, which is served by several carriers, including United (800-864-8331; www.united.com).
▶ **Best Time to Visit**: Mid-May to mid-September.
▶ **Level of Difficulty**: There are climbs for people of varied abilities, though individuals hoping to summit should have a level of experience . . . and remember, many of the ascents here are considered more difficult than their rating.
▶ **Guides**: There are several older guidebooks available, including *Devils Tower National Monument Climbing Handbook* (Richard Guilmette, Renee Carrier, and Steve Gardiner). Devils Tower Climbing (www.devilstowerclimbing.com) offers guided climbs.
▶ **Accommodations**: The Belle Fourche River Campground (www.nps.gov/deto) has forty-six sites available on a first-come/first-served basis. Devils Tower Lodge (307-467-5267; www.devilstowerlodge.com) offers fine accommodations . . . and camping in the yard.

GRAND TETON NATIONAL PARK

RECOMMENDED BY **Rob Hess**

The Teton Range, just north of Jackson, Wyoming, is not home to America's tallest mountains, though its peaks may be the country's most recognizable. Rising abruptly from the valley floor, its distinctive jagged tops are icons of the eponymous national park—and perhaps even the American West. Grand Teton, which measures 13,770 feet at its summit and rises some seven thousand feet from the valley floor, looms over it all.

"Anyone who has driven through Jackson Hole and looked to the west at Grand Teton can't help but wonder, 'What would it be like to be on top of that thing?'" Rob Hess began. "Most don't have an opportunity, but a few do make it."

Stretching forty miles and including thirteen peaks that eclipse eleven thousand feet, the Tetons are a paradise for mountaineers and rock climbers alike. "There's a broad array of high-quality climbing experiences here," Rob continued. "Some are day climbs, some are overnight, and some are a few nights. A couple of the single-day climbs are in Cascade Canyon. First you take a boat across Jenny Lake, then hike into the crags. One route we like is Guide's Wall, which is an hour's walk. Generally it's a six-pitch climb, though there's some variation. It can be anywhere from 5.6 to 5.9, depending on how we do it. There are some moderate towers at Ice Point and Storm Point. Symmetry Spire, at the north end of Jenny Lake, also has some nice objectives than can be done as a day trip.

"We operate a high camp on the route to the summit of Grand Teton, and this is home base for those climbing the Garnet Towers. The camp is at eleven thousand feet, and it's a rigorous hike up—you gain four thousand feet over six hours. But you don't have to carry much gear, as the camp at Corbet is well stocked. From here, there are many options. The Watchtower is nearby, and there are a variety of objectives here. Corkscrew [5.8+] is a spectacular six-pitch route. Fairshare Tower is equally close by. The route here [Crawl

OPPOSITE:
Though it is not the park's most technical climb, reaching the top of Grand Teton is still a prized accomplishment.

221

Along the Watchtower, 5.8] is eight pitches, and a little more mountaineering oriented. If you hike down farther past Watchtower, you'll reach Irene's Arête. It's a striking tower when you look up from the meadows, one of the Tetons' most iconic climbs, with clean cracks, airy, and continuous pitches, all among spectacular surroundings. [It's named for Teton great Irene Beardsley (Ortenburger) who discovered this prize with John Dietschy in 1957.] Finally, there's Red Sentinel, about twenty minutes from the camp. The Regular Route [5.7] is only three pitches, but one of the most dramatic pinnacles in the park. The first pitch props you on an arête, the next takes you to the north side of the pinnacle, and everything drops away. Then there's one more pitch to the summit. When you rappel off, you're dropping 180 feet, three quarters of which are free-hanging. It's very dramatic."

A different adventure awaits on Mount Moran, which is on the northern end of the range, a bit apart from the other Teton peaks. "This is a three-day trip, more alpine with some rock climbing," Rob described. "The first day, you canoe across String and Leigh Lakes to the base of the mountain, and hike a couple thousand feet up to the CMC campsite. The next day, you climb the mountain. It starts with some scrambling to reach the top of a little tower called Drizzlepuss. From here, we downclimb into a notch. Then we continue on the CMC route [5.5] to the top. There's lots of variation. It's a very scenic trip on a less-traveled section of the Tetons."

Though it's not technically demanding, many climbers visiting the Tetons may still wish to knock off Grand Teton itself. For a group with less climbing experience, Rob recommends setting aside four days to successfully summit. Day one is the hike up the Lupine Meadows Trail to Corbet High Camp. Day two is about getting everyone comfortable with the technical aspects of rock climbing. "To make it to the top of Grand Teton, climbers need to execute three feats—technical scrambling, pitched climbing, and one rappel," Rob explained. "We walk through these techniques on nearby Garnet Towers. We'll often do our multi-pitch climb and rappel practice on Crawl Along the Watchtower. On day three, we usually get up by three A.M., have a good breakfast, and then start walking with headlamps. We descend to the climber's trail and then begin gaining elevation. A fifty-foot fixed rope takes us to Lower Saddle. We're usually here by five or 5:30. From here, it's on toward Upper Saddle. At this point there's some scrambling; it's not especially difficult, but the consequences of a fall are serious, so people are roped up. We're generally on Upper Saddle—thirteen thousand feet—by seven or 7:30, and the air is warming with the sunlight. At this point, we don our stack ropes and tie in for the two or three pitched climbs we have ahead. The last two hundred feet are an exposed, though fairly easy, scramble. Between 8:30 and 10:30, we're on the summit. On a clear day, you can view fourteen different mountain ranges in four states!"

When you're leaving Jackson Hole, you'll be able to look up with pride.

ROB HESS is one of only several guides nationwide who is certified by the International Federation of Mountain Guide Associations (IFMGA), the foremost guide certification organization worldwide. He was the third American to climb Mount Everest without oxygen. Rob has also successfully guided Broad Peak (26,440 feet) in the Karakoram of Pakistan. He is the technical director of the American Mountain Guides Association, and in 2007 received their Outstanding Guide of the Year Award. Rob is an owner of Jackson Hole Mountain Guides.

If You Go

▶ **Getting There:** Jackson Hole Airport is served by Delta (800-221-1212; www.delta.com) and United (800-864-8331; www.united.com). Some visitors will fly into Salt Lake City (served by most major carriers) and drive to Jackson, approximately six hours.

▶ **Best Time to Visit**: Guided climbs of Grand Teton are led from June through mid-September. Climbs are weather-dependent. Visit www.nps.gov/grte regarding other hiking opportunities in Grand Teton National Park.

▶ **Level of Difficulty**: There's a broad range of climbs here, from 5.5 up. Even inexperienced climbers can summit Grand Teton with the help of a guide.

Guides/Outfitters: Several outfitters lead climbs of Grand Teton, including Jackson Hole Mountain Guides (800-239-7642; www.jhmg.com).

▶ **Accommodations**: American Alpine Club's Grand Teton Climbers' Ranch (https://lodging.americanalpineclub.org) provides affordable digs. Camping options in the park are highlighted at www.nps.gov/grte. The Jackson Hole Chamber of Commerce (307-733-3316; www.jacksonholechamber.com) lists lodging options in town.

Library of Congress Control Number: 2019939759

ISBN: 978-1-4197-4292-7
eISBN: 978-1-68335-889-3

Text copyright © 2020 Chris Santella

Photograph credits: pages 2, 120: © Carter Clark; 8, 88: © Andrew Burr; 10, 65: © Garrett Bradley; 14, 174:
© Tim Kemple; 16, 18, 23, 48, 56, 61, 72, 92, 96, 108, 124, 130, 150, 170, 178, 186, 192, 208, 216: © Jim Thornburg;
22: © John Price; 26: © Chester Voyage/Alamy Stock Photo; 30: © T. Bok; 34: © Brendan Hung/Shutterstock;
38: © Kletterzentrum Innsbruck; 42: © All Canada Photos/Alamy Stock Photo; 52: © Jeff Deikis; 68: © Prisma by
Dukas Presseagentur GmbH/Alamy Stock Photo; 76: © Westend61 GmbH/Alamy Stock Photo; 84: © Andy Day/
Alamy Stock Photo; 100: © Sawtooth Mountain Guides; 105: © Tim Bohman; 112: © Cavan/Alamy Stock Photo;
117: Benjamin Chad Smith; 134: © Maria Nasif/Alamy Stock Photo; 138: © Nathan Bancroft; 142: © Andy Chasteen;
146: © Glen Harris; 154: © Emma Wood/Alamy Stock Photo; 158: © Scott Noy; 162: © Pius Lee; 166: © Wordley
Calvo Stock; 182: © Cultura Creative (RF)/Alamy Stock Photo; 196: © Rachel Ross; 201: © Robert Crum/Alamy
Stock Photo; 204: © Dan Brayak; 212: © Nick Wilkes; 220: © Brad Mitchell/Alamy Stock Photo

Jacket © 2020 Abrams

Editor: Samantha Weiner
Designer: Anna Christian
Production Manager: Kathleen Gaffney

This book was composed in Interstate, Scala, and Village.

Printed and bound in China
10 9 8 7 6 5 4 3 2 1

Abrams Image books are available at special discounts when purchased in quantity for premiums and
promotions as well as fundraising or educational use. Special editions can also be created to specification.
For details, contact specialsales@abramsbooks.com or the address below.

Abrams Image® is a registered trademark of Harry N. Abrams, Inc.

ABRAMS The Art of Books
195 Broadway, New York, NY 10007
abramsbooks.com